HISTORY

OF

THE HUMANE SOCIETY

OF THE

Commonwealth of Massachusetts:

WITH

A SELECTED LIST OF PREMIUMS

AWARDED BY THE TRUSTEES, FROM ITS COMMENCEMENT TO THE PRESENT TIME,

AND A

LIST OF THE MEMBERS AND OFFICERS.

PREPARED BY DIRECTION OF THE TRUSTEES.

BOSTON:
PRESS OF T. R. MARVIN & SON, 49 FEDERAL STREET.
1876.

In accordance with the precedents of the Society, a vote of the Trustees was passed April 7, 1876, directing F. B. Crowninshield, President, C. A. Curtis, Treasurer, and A. T. Perkins, Secretary, to have the History and By-laws of the Society reprinted, together with a List of the Officers and Members, and a Selected List of the Premiums awarded. The following statement is by them, on behalf of the Trustees, respectfully presented to the members of the Society, and to others interested in its objects. They have reprinted the History of the Society almost exactly as it came from the hands of Messrs. Francis Parkman, John Homans and John L. Gardner, in 1845, making only such additions as the lapse of thirty years has rendered necessary.

F. B. CROWNINSHIELD.
CALEB A. CURTIS.
AUGUSTUS T. PERKINS.

HISTORY.

"THE HUMANE SOCIETY OF THE COMMONWEALTH OF MASSACHUSETTS," was instituted in 1786. Its origin at that time, or the immediate occasion of its formation, was the result of an interview between the late Rev. Dr. James Freeman, Dr. Aaron Dexter, Royall Tyler, Esq., and Dr. Moyes, a gentleman from England, then residing in Boston, who, though blind from his childhood, had distinguished himself by his scientific attainments, and by his zeal for the interests of philanthropy. In conversing on the various charitable institutions established in Great Britain, Dr. Moyes, as we learn from a document already published, "suggested the outlines of a plan of a society, similar to that of the British Royal Humane Society, incorporated in 1774, in imitation of one in Holland, to restore to life persons apparently dead," &c. The proposal engaged the earnest attention of the above-named gentlemen, who communicated it to the Hon. James Bowdoin, afterwards its first President, and obtaining with his the cordial concurrence of several other influential citizens, it was resolved at once to carry it into effect. Subscriptions were opened for the establishment of a fund, and a meeting of the subscribers, thenceforth its members, being held at "The Bunch of Grapes Tavern," in State Street, a Society was duly organized, January 5, 1786, by the appointment of officers, in number and description precisely the same as have been annually elected from that to the present time.

The Society was incorporated in 1791, John Hancock, Esq., being then the Governor of the Commonwealth. And "the end and design of the institution," as expressed in the Act, is "for the recovery of persons who meet with such accidents as to produce in them the appearance of death, *and for promoting the cause of humanity, by pursuing such means, from time to time, as shall have for their object the preservation of human life, and the alleviation of its miseries.*"

The formation of charitable societies, now so common, was at that time of very rare occurrence; * and among a people just tasting the first fruits of their independence, and engaged in establishing their own institutions, excited no common interest. The excellence of the objects proposed, approving themselves at once to

* Excepting the Marine Society, founded in 1742; the "Massachusetts Congregational Charitable Society," incorporated in 1786; and the "Society for Propagating the Gospel among the Indians, and others, in North America," incorporated in 1787, no charitable associations, originating among our own citizens, had as yet been formed. The Boston Dispensary was of much later origin; and the only exceptions that can be adduced to the statements above made, are the institution of "The Quarterly Charity Lecture," and the Boston Almshouse.

every enlightened mind ; the example of a most flourishing society for the same purpose in Great Britain, commanding the general as well as the royal patronage, united, perhaps, with a disposition in our community, early developed, and still active, to delight itself in things new, gave to the beginnings of this Society a marked distinction. Nor did this cease with its earliest days. For a series of years, the most respectable and influential of our citizens, in different parts of the Commonwealth, were enrolled among its members. The most distinguished professional gentlemen, lay as well as clerical, were selected for its orators ; liberal contributions to its funds showed the sense entertained of the importance of its design; while its anniversaries, in the pleasant month of June, which the Executive, with the legislature of the State, then in session, repeatedly adjourned to attend, were honored by crowded assemblies, and attended by somewhat of the "pomp and circumstance" belonging to those days, but which, with familiarity and changes in the habits of society have now passed away.*

* The first Catalogue of the members of the Society was appended to Dr. Lathrop's Discourse at the first Anniversary, 1787, and contains one hundred and forty names. The Catalogue of 1810 exhibits the names of six hundred and eleven members, residents of various parts of the Commonwealth, besides a list of honorary members, among whom are Drs. Fothergill and Lettsom, with the Earl of Stamford and others of Great Britain, Dr. Baron of Calcutta, Dr. Rush of Philadelphia, and various distinguished gentlemen in other parts of the United States.

Members were at first, and afterwards, for a long series of years, admitted only on the recommendation of a Trustee, or some other member. And in instances as late as 1824, were on their request as formally dismissed, or in other words released from the payment of an annual subscription.

No sooner was the Society formed, than application for the aids it contemplates was presented. Of the first meeting of the Trustees, at the house of Dr. John Warren, February, 1786, one month from the time of its organization, the following is a part of the record.

> "It being made to appear to the Trustees, that Mr. Andrew Sloane had, since the institution of the Society, by a signal exertion, saved a lad from drowning, who had fallen into the ice through the Mill-Dam: — *Voted,* That said Sloane be paid the sum of twenty-eight shillings, agreeably to the fourteenth article."

As this was the first premium adjudged, followed soon after by one of a similar description, so the first instance of resuscitation communicated was that of a child of a painter in Boston, who, in October of 1787, fell into a deep cistern, and was taken out apparently dead; but by the persevering use of the methods recommended by the Society, under the direction of an intelligent neighbor, was completely recovered. Such were the beginnings of a long series of cases, amounting to many hundreds in number, which, in their various degrees of human peril and suffering on the one hand, of heroic exertion and humanity on the other, have awakened the sympathies and obtained the premiums of the Society.

Of other objects soon engaging their attention, was the erection of huts on exposed portions of the coast, for the shelter of shipwrecked seamen. To this, however, as forming an important part of its present arrangements, we shall have occasion to advert more particularly hereafter. In immediate connection with this, was a proposal, in 1788, to erect houses, and even to settle families on the Isle of Sables, near Cape Breton, for the protection of the many, in each year, who were wrecked on that desolate spot. But the funds of the Society being wholly inadequate to an undertaking of such magnitude, a committee was appointed to present an address to His Excellency Governor Hancock, who was a proprietor of a large part of the island, and to request his recommendation of the object either to the legislature of the State, or to the Congress of the United States, as he might deem most expedient. The Governor complied with the request, by sending a message to the General Court; and a communication was at the same time held with some influential citizens of Halifax, (Nova Scotia,) near to which, also, Cape Sable is situated. But of the results of these measures, the records of the Society do not furnish information.*

At this period, and for many years subsequent, it was usual with the Trustees to make an annual visit to the

* The following article, as it shows the importance of the matter, is extracted from a Halifax newspaper of July, 1787:—

"The number of vessels continually wrecked on Cape Sable Island makes it highly necessary, that some steps should be taken by government to settle a family or two there. The expense could not be great; and there cannot be a doubt that the New England States would cheerfully join with the government here, and the underwriters, in a measure, by which their interests, and the lives of so many valuable fellow-creatures might be preserved."

islands in the harbor, in order to inspect their huts. On these occasions the President was authorized to invite the Governor, with distinguished strangers, and such other guests as he should deem proper. On one of these anniversaries, Governor Hancock being by indisposition unable to attend, ordered a salute to be fired in honor of the Society, as their boat passed the Castle William; for which courtesy he received their vote of thanks. The Trustees had the frequent mortification, as will hereafter be seen, to find their huts plundered, or the materials destroyed. But the painful duties of these visitations seem to have been abundantly relieved by a measure of festivity not unknown in those days to the fathers, and even to the highest dignitaries of the Commonwealth, under the burdens of their official duties. And probably it was in some observation of the tendencies of a generous hospitality to profusion, that the Trustees have from time to time adopted, for their own direction, some very judicious resolves, in the shape of sumptuary laws; of which, if the effects, with the usual slowness attending this species of regulation, have not been manifest to themselves, they will hope that they may yet be tasted to their fullest extent by their successors.

As this Society was for many years one of only three or four charitable institutions within Massachusetts, proposals were occasionally made to engraft other objects upon its original purpose. Among these we find a communication from the Rev. Dr. Belknap, the distinguished biographer and historian, suggesting that some provision be made for the sick-poor, and particularly for exposed children. A large committee, of whom were Judge Lowell, Dr. Belknap, Judge Sullivan, and Thomas Russell, Esq., were appointed from the Society at large to consider and report upon the subject, who recommended a consultation with the Medical faculty, in order most effectually to provide "for the sick-poor, for the assistance of lying-in women, and for foundlings." They also reported in favor of procuring subscriptions for a public DISPENSARY; and thus probably originated that excellent institution, which for now more than fifty years has been the instrument of great good in our city.

The condition and sufferings of American citizens, then in captivity among the Algerines, was in 1794, a subject of deep interest. At a meeting of the Trustees, May 5th, of that year, the President and four other gentlemen were selected as a committee to apply to the General Court for a brief to collect money in their favor. They received, also, a letter from the Vice-President of the United States, with several letters from the captives themselves in Algiers, addressed to the American Consul. But upon mature deliberation it was deemed expedient to defer any active measures for the present.

In the course of two or three successive seasons several deaths had occurred to persons bathing in Cambridge river, particularly among the students of the College. A committee, of whom were Dr. John Warren and Dr. Dexter, was therefore appointed "to confer with a committee of the College and the inhabitants of Cambridge upon the expediency and practicability of erecting a bath upon that dangerous river, for the purpose of preventing such accidents;" and to this object the Society appropriated one hundred and fifty dollars.*

The yellow fever having prevailed in Boston, Philadelphia, and other of our cities during the summer and autumn of 1798, the Trustees offered a piece of plate of the value of fifty dollars "for the greatest number of important and well-substantiated facts instrumental in giving origin to the yellow fever in the United States." The premium was awarded to Samuel Brown, M. D., and his dissertation was published at the expense of the Society.

As might have been anticipated, or rather as experience made probable, many mistaken or deceptive applications were made to the Society for its rewards, in cases either not coming within its province, or when, in the actual relieving of a sufferer no danger had been incurred, or with collusion and intention to deceive,

* For some measures, which the Trustees also adopted at a later period for the encouragement of a swimming-school in Boston, specially for the benefit of the boys of the public schools, by inviting the co-operation of the Mayor and Aldermen, and appropriating one hundred dollars for the purpose, see Note, under the Catalogue of Premiums awarded.

when the whole story was a fabrication, and no danger to any party existed. Of this latter species of baseness, as when claims were made for meritorious efforts in drawing a man out of the water, who, it appeared upon inquiry, "*had never fallen into the water at all*," some few instances are of faithful record in our Appendix. With a view to discourage all such plotters, as well as to preclude fruitless applications, the Trustees did, in 1799, cause public notice to be made, both of the proper objects of their institution, and of the nature of the services which they considered as alone entitled to a reward. Signal exertions, not merely those which common humanity would demand, and which it would be disgraceful in any human being to refuse, coupled with personal exposure and danger, are represented in their Resolutions as indispensable. "Signal exertion," as is expressed, "includes the endangering of life, or incurring some damage by impairing the health, or injuring apparel, or other property."

In November, 1801, the Rev. Dr. Parker informed the Trustees, "that a gentleman had made an offer of four hundred dollars to the Humane Society for the purpose of erecting a building for those persons who are so unfortunate as to become insane." The subject was referred by the Trustees to the Society at their semi-annual meeting, in December, who appointed a large committee to consider the subject and report at a future meeting.

This appears to have been the first suggestion of a subject of great moment, which afterwards engaged much of the attention of the Society. No measures, however, seem to have been adopted in relation to it until 1816, when, at the meeting of the Trustees in October of that year, a communication was received from the Trustees of the Massachusetts General Hospital, inviting attention to the subject, and submitting certain proposals to our consideration. The proposals themselves were not adopted; but at the meeting of the Trustees on November 6th, the President, Dr. Dexter, communicated the following letter: —

To the President and Trustees of the Humane Society:

Gentlemen: We, the subscribers, members of the Humane Society, actuated solely by a desire to promote a cause most interesting to humanity, and of a nature consistent with the general design of our institution, respectfully request that the funds of the Society, so far as they are disposable by the Trustees, may be applied to the encouragement of the Hospital for Lunatics, proposed to be established in this town, or its vicinity.

This letter was signed by George Cabot and thirty-four other members of the Society, and it was unanimously

Voted, That the Trustees do authorize the Treasurer to subscribe five thousand dollars in behalf of the Society towards the establishment of an Hospital for insane persons.

It was also *Voted,* That the Rev. Charles Lowell, Samuel Parkman, Esq., and Dr. Spooner, be a committee to confer with the Trustees of the "Massachusetts General Hospital," and request the aid of that Corporation in the proposed establishment.

This committee conferred agreeably to their appointment. The offer of the Trustees was accepted by the General Hospital Corporation on certain terms and conditions mutually agreed; the Treasurer subscribed the five thousand dollars; and "thus," says the history of 1829, "the Humane Society laid the foundation of the Asylum for the Insane."

At a stated meeting of the Trustees in July, 1820, an additional donation, of seven hundred and fifty dollars, was made to the "Massachusetts General Hospital," on the same terms and conditions as the previous sum. And in August, 1824, upon the Report of a committee, consisting of Rev. Dr. Lowell, Dr. J. C. Warren, and Judge Thacher, appointed to consider the expediency of affording further aid, it was unanimously voted to appropriate "a sum sufficient to support six free or charity beds, within that institution, on condition that the occupation of these beds be at the disposal of the officers of this Society, namely, the President, Vice-Presidents, Secretaries, and Treasurer, each one bed; and, provided, that the number of charity beds, previously existing in the Hospital, be not diminished in consequence of this donation, but that the beds supported by the Humane Society be considered as added to those existing." This grant was limited to three years, but, upon the expiration of that term, was renewed on like conditions, and so continued, as will appear, until 1834.

In September, 1830, Rev. Dr. Lowell, John Heard, Esq., and Dr. Hayward, were appointed to consider and report the expediency of appropriating an additional sum from the funds of this Society in aid of some other humane and charitable object. Accordingly, in the following December, they reported that "they knew of no object more deserving, or more needed in the present condition of the community, than an establishment for Lying-in women; and proposed that *five thousand dollars* be appropriated in aid of this object, on condition that twelve thousand dollars more be raised, by subscription, within six months." The committee advert, in their Report, to the fact we have already stated, that the idea of a similar institution was suggested at an early period of this Society; that with the advancing population of the city, the want of such an asylum had become the more urgent; and that the object itself was altogether in accordance with the general design of this Society,—which is, as expressed in the Act of incorporation, "the preservation of human life and the alleviation of its miseries." This Report was accepted, and the same committee were authorized to carry it into full effect.

The Trustees of the Massachusetts General Hospital, having proffered their aid towards the same object, a conference was held with a committee of that Board. Another and larger committee, composed of five of our Trustees, was appointed for the collecting of subscriptions, and inviting the co-operation of the "Massachusetts Charitable Society." Both these objects having been accomplished, the result was the establishment, in 1832, of "The Boston Lying-in Hospital," as it is now conducted. The Act of incorporation, afterwards obtained, reserves to this Society the right of visiting, or exercising a supervising power over its affairs. In virtue of this provision, two of its Board of Trustees are annually appointed from the Trustees of the Humane Society. In January, 1834, three hundred dollars were appropriated from our funds, to the support of three free beds in the Lying-in Asylum; and the same grant was continued annually, until 1838, when, on application from the Directors of the Lying-in Hospital, for additional aid, to meet some pressing exigencies, a donation was made of nine hundred dollars; it being understood, that this special grant should be regarded as exempting the Society, for the future, from any annual contributions in support of that institution.

In consequence of the provision from our funds, for free beds in the "Lying-in Asylum," it was deemed expedient that the number of beds, provided by us, in the General Hospital, should be diminished. Accordingly, since 1834, three hundred dollars only, instead of six hundred, have been annually appropriated for beds in this latter institution. These are under the charge of the President, who gives orders, as occasion arises, for the admission to them of proper subjects.

Applications are very frequently made. It is seldom that these, our free beds, are at any time unoccupied; and during the term of twenty years, that has now elapsed since this excellent provision was adopted, a very large number of sick-poor have partaken of its benefits.*

HUTS FOR SHELTER.

At an early period of the Society, as has been already seen, the erection of huts for the shelter and comfort of persons unfortunately shipwrecked was among the objects of its attention. Within a few months after its organization appropriations were made for this purpose. Several huts, on exposed parts of the Massachusetts coast, have been from time to time erected, repaired, or renewed, as circumstances required, furnished with fuel and other articles most needful for the exhausted mariner. At no period have the Trustees lost sight of this object; but as the number of dwelling houses along the coast has very much increased during the last twenty years, it has not been necessary to add to the

* It appears from the records of the Massachusetts General Hospital, which were carefully examined by the Superintendent, for the purpose, at the request of the committee, that, during the twenty years, from 1825 to 1845, "there have been admitted to the free beds of the Humane Society, on order of its officers, 171 patients, who remained in the Hospital 1054 weeks, making the average time for each patient, six weeks and one day.

Besides these, others appear to have been admitted, and to have occupied our charity beds, "by the order of subscribers," so that the whole number probably, exceeds 200. Since 1845, the Society having regularly continued to subscribe for free beds in the Hospital, the number who have received assistance from that source, up to 1876, is very large.

number of our huts in the same ratio as we have increased our life-saving stations ; and, of the huts now existing and their respective locations, the following is the enumeration :

At	NANTASKET LONG BEACH, . .	one.
"	NAUSET BEACH, ...	"
"	MILK ISLAND, CAPE ANN, . .	"
"	ORLEANS BEACH, ...	"
"	WELLFLEET, ...	"

At Nantucket, also, there are three huts, under the charge of individuals of that Island.*

We regret for the sake of our common humanity to be compelled to say, that neither the sacredness of the charity, nor the urgent necessity to the shipwrecked sufferers of the materials supplied ; nor yet the thought of the bitter disappointment and distress, which the want of them at such a crisis must occasion, have protected these humble but hallowed abodes from plunder.

* It was usual with the Trustees, in their arrangements for the Huts, to engage the assistance, or to avail themselves of the counsel, of judicious individuals, most conversant with the locations of the coast. Many valuable services of this nature were rendered and gratefully acknowledged. At a meeting in October, 1802, it appears that the late Rev. Dr. Freeman, having been requested, by a preceding vote, to "inquire for the most important places on Cape Cod, where small Huts may be erected to receive shipwrecked seamen, and to determine how many be necessary," and having fulfilled this commission to the great satisfaction of the Trustees, it was

Voted, "That the thanks of the Society be given to the Rev. Mr. James Freeman for his very judicious and accurate report, respecting the Huts on Cape Cod ; and, that two thousand copies be printed in a large type, and distributed in several parts of this Commonwealth, for the benefit of seafaring men."

Scarcely had one been erected on Lovell's Island, in 1789, before it was found necessary to offer rewards for the discovery of the perpetrators of so base an outrage. And even to the present, in instances not a few, have the Trustees found themselves obliged to repair the wastes of this peculiarly cruel and wanton depredation, in comparison of which, as was indignantly said by an eloquent preacher on one of the annual celebrations, "common robbery is righteousness." *

LIFE BOATS.

It has also been a favorite and highly important object of the Society to provide LIFE BOATS as among the surest means of preserving human life in its most exposed and threatening positions; alike valuable to them who are in peril, and to them who are willing to attempt their rescue. Accordingly, as early as October, 1807, one was completed under the direction of a skillful committee, and with the advice of some experienced mariners, was stationed at Cohasset, where it remained until 1813.

The honor of this inestimable invention belongs to Henry Greathead, Esq., a native of South Shields in England. And though like many others of the most valuable discoveries, which science and art, quickened by humanity, have made for the benefit of our race, it

* Rev. Thomas Thacher, in his Anniversary Discourse of June, 1800.

failed at first of attracting notice; yet such was the experience of its utility, that it at length obtained the attention of the British Parliament, who voted to its inventor the sum of twelve hundred pounds sterling, while two thousand more were presented him by individuals to encourage the building of his Boats. In several instances one hundred pounds were subscribed by Humane Societies for the same purpose; and the gift of a costly diamond ring was presented to Mr. Greathead, by the Emperor of Russia.

At different periods of our own Society, since that already referred to, measures have been adopted in reference to this object. Particularly at the meeting of the Board in January, 1840, a committee was appointed to carry it into execution. But the funds of the Society not admitting of a large expenditure for this single, however desirable, purpose, it was with high satisfaction that at the meeting of April, in the same year, the Trustees received an official communication of a Resolve, passed by the Legislature of the State, of which the following is a copy.

Commonwealth of Massachusetts.

In the year one thousand eight hundred and forty.

Resolved, That there be allowed and paid out of the Treasury of the Commonwealth, to the President and Trustees of the Massachusetts Humane Society, the sum of five thousand dollars, for the purpose of furnishing Life Boats, to be stationed at the most exposed parts of the seacoast within this Commonwealth, and that a warrant be drawn therefor. And that the said Society be requested to report to the Governor and Council their expenditure of the funds appropriated by this Resolve, together with the number and stations of the boats.

House of Representatives, March 21, 1840, passed.

ROBERT C. WINTHROP, *Speaker*.

In the Senate, March 21, 1840.

DANIEL P. KING, *President*.

Approved,

MARCUS MORTON.

With this liberal and effective aid, altogether worthy of an enlightened commonwealth, the Society was at once enabled to accomplish its desired purpose. And under the superintendence of the President, Benjamin Rich, Esq., and of the late lamented Henry Oxnard, eleven boats, together with one provided from the Society's own fund, were completed, and an official Report, of which the following is a copy, was at the ensuing session of the Legislature, agreeably to the terms of the Resolve, presented to the Governor and Council.

BOSTON, January 4, 1841.

To his Excellency JOHN DAVIS, *and to the Honorable Council:*

The Trustees of the Humane Society of Massachusetts beg leave to present to your Excellency, and to the Honorable Council, the following Report, as submitted to their own body by a committee chosen from themselves to carry into effect the above-mentioned Resolve.

The committee, in addition to a Life Boat provided by the Humane Society, have built eleven, which are stationed in the following places: One boat at Nantucket, one at Martha's Vineyard, three at Cape Cod, which are arranged by John Atkins, Esq., with the approbation of the Selectmen ; one at Cohasset, one at Nantasket Beach, one at Lynn, one at Gloucester, one at Sandy Bay, one at Plumb Island, under the care of the Humane Society at Newburyport ; with one on Scituate Beach, which will be paid for by the Massachusetts Humane Society.

The whole number of boats thus provided is twelve ; all of which are furnished with oars, buckets, and four bars of iron for ballast. These can be taken out when it is necessary to transport the boats to any distance. A house twenty feet long, eight feet and a half wide, shingled on the top and battened on the sides, has been built for each boat.

The following, may it please your Excellency and the Honorable Council, is a part of the letter addressed, in the name of the Trustees, to the Selectmen of one of the towns within which the boats are stationed, ana signed by our President, Benjamin Rich, Esq. Similar notices were given to the authorities of the other towns.

BOSTON, August 10. 1840.

To Hon. GEORGE B. UPTON, *and the Selectmen of Nantucket :*

Gentlemen : With the money granted by the State, the Massachusetts Humane Society have a Life Boat finished, which they wish placed in the best situation to relieve shipwrecked mariners on your Island. They wish you to select ten active men, one of whom to be appointed as chairman, (sending in their names, which are to be recorded in the books of the Society,) to take charge of said boat, any five or six of whom being present can manage her. But their services must be considered as granted voluntarily for humane and charitable purposes. And whenever any meritorious act is performed by the volunteers in the boat, in rescuing lives, they shall be suitably rewarded on a full representation of the same to the Society.

It is necessary that a suitable house should be built to protect the boat from the weather ; the bill of which will be paid on presentment.

[Here follows a detailed statement of the cost of the boats, and of the articles supplied, all included with the above, in the Report to the Council, but unnecessary here to repeat.]

From the foregoing statement it will appear that, of the five thousand dollars received by the Trustees from the treasury of the Commonwealth, there have been expended for the purposes for which it was granted, four thousand nine hundred and sixty-two dollars, seventy-two cents, leaving a balance unexpended of said grant of thirty-seven dollars twenty-eight cents; which, together with the sum of two hundred dollars received from the Newburyport Marine Society, leaves a balance of two hundred thirty-seven dollars twenty-eight cents in the hands of our Treasurer for the above-named purposes.

All which is respectfully submitted.

By direction of the Trustees,

FRANCIS PARKMAN,
HENRY OXNARD.

At a subsequent meeting of the Trustees, the following letter from the Council, in reply to the Report, was presented, and ordered to be placed on file.

To Rev. FRANCIS PARKMAN,
and HENRY OXNARD, Esq.

Gentlemen : The Committee of the Council, to whom was referred the Report of the Humane Society, of their expenditure of five thousand dollars granted by Resolve, March 21, 1840, have received the same and found it satisfactory. They respectfully suggest, that advantages would arise from publication of the stations of each boat in the newspapers, as it would also give satisfaction to the members of the Legislature. The points or places where the boats are stationed should be accurately defined, so that shipwrecked vessels might direct their course, if in their power, to such places. The Committee would be happy to confer with you upon this subject, if you should think any advantage would arise therefrom.

With great respect,

Jos. Grennell,
By order of the Committee.

Council Chamber, January 12, 1841.

Agreeably to the above suggestion, publication was duly made of the numbers and stations of the Life Boats; and an accurate list, as they are at present located, will be found in the Appendix.

In the session of 1841, an additional grant, of thirteen hundred and fifty dollars, was made by the Legislature; and an acknowledgment of the same, with a statement of the expenditure, was presented, as before, to the Governor and Council, by the President of the Society.

The equipment of the Society at the present time, [1876,] exactly ninety years from its foundation, is very complete. It has sixty-two boats, commanded by experienced officers, and manned by volunteer crews, composed of the boldest and most enterprising men on the seaboard. These boats are located at the most exposed points on the coast of Massachusetts, ranged along from Ipswich River on the north, to the Island of Cuttahunk on the southern boundary of the State.

Fifteen mortars are placed where the rocks or sand bars project into the sea, so that if a vessel should go ashore within three hundred yards of the land, her crew would have a fair chance of being saved by lines thrown over them, as no boats could live in the cross-seas which are so terrible at these shallow and most dangerous places.

Mr. R. B. Forbes, Vice-President of the Society, with the assistance of Colonel Laidley, United States Army, and Mr. C. A. Curtis, one of the Trustees, aided by Captain George Dewey, United States Navy, have recently been making a series of experiments in casting lines from rifled guns, with such success that the great range of five hundred yards has been obtained. If this range can be relied upon, it is probable that rifled guns will be substituted for mortars at such places as Peaked Hill Bars, and others of the more dangerous points along the coast.

The officers of the Army and Navy of the United States, stationed in Massachusetts, have always shown the greatest interest in the Society, and have from time to time rendered most valuable services to it.

The inhabitants of the State,—women as well as men, as our records show—have exhibited instances of heroic courage, and have displayed humane characteristics which have been surpassed by no other people.

Owing to the exertions of the Trustees of the Society from time to time, especially those of William Appleton and Samuel Hooper, both of whom were members of Congress from Boston, the usefulness of the Society was so demonstrated to the United States Government, that grants at different times, amounting to many thousand dollars, have been made and expended in boats, huts, rafts, mortars, and other apparatus, as the settlement of our accounts with the government show — by means of which hundreds of valuable lives have been saved, and supplementary life-saving stations have been established under the supervision of government officers of the most efficient character. The State of Massachusetts has at times, when the needs of the Society were greater than they are at this moment, generously assisted it with very considerable sums of money.

The Society has the utmost reason to acknowledge a paternal Providence, and to congratulate a benevolent community on the good already accomplished, and the far greater good to be anticipated from these wise provisions up to 1845, one of these boats alone, — that stationed at Hull,—had been the means of saving thirty-six lives and the number rescued by our life boats there and elsewhere may be counted by hundreds. And if the inhabitants of these and other exposed portions of our coast have found demands upon their heroism and humanity, frequent and urgent beyond what might seem their due proportion, they will find, we are persuaded, corresponding satisfaction, in having been the instruments, under heaven, of delivering from death and giving back to domestic love, to friendship, usefulness, and shall we not hope, to "newness of life," their rescued and grateful fellow-citizens.

If we look only to the special purpose for which the Society was established, "the preservation of human life," without including in the estimate the various kindred objects which at different periods have engaged its attention and been aided by its funds, we find ample testimony of its beneficial influence. It would be difficult to exhibit with any exactness of numbers the individuals, whose names in the course of the ninety years since its institution have been enrolled on its records, either as the instruments or objects of the humanity it encourages; who have saved, or have themselves been saved from "going down to death." *

* At the anniversary of "The Royal Humane Society," in 1804, it was stated that since its institution in 1774, a period of only thirty years, two thousand eight hundred and fifty-nine persons of all ages and conditions had been recorded in its books as rescued from imminent peril and restored to life; and that four thousand five hundred and eighty-seven individuals had been rewarded by its funds for humane exertions. It was customary, also, at those anniversaries, to assemble as many as could be collected of the persons thus recovered, who went in procession and were seated together in a conspicuous part of the church. On one occasion, the numbers of this singular company exceeded seven hundred; and their anthem of thanksgiving was that of the healed King of Judah: "The grave cannot praise Thee: Death cannot celebrate Thee: they that go down to the pit cannot hope for Thy truth. But the living, the living, he shall praise Thee, as I do this day."

A Hymn was composed by Mrs. Morton, for the anniversaries of our own Society, one stanza of which is supposed to be sung by the persons recovered. The Hymn itself was repeatedly sung by Mrs. Graupner and others, as appears in the notices of the occasion, at the time; but we believe that in no instance was there an assemblage of the persons restored.

The following is the well-known stanza: —

"Since twice to die is ours alone,
And twice the breath of life to see,
Oh! may we, prostrate at Thy throne,
Devote our second lives to Thee."

But when we add to these the far wider circle of kindred and friends, of fathers and mothers, of wives and sisters, whose distracting fears or speechless anguish have been changed to exulting joy, there rises to our view a countless multitude, who have had reason to bless its instrumentality. To appreciate the value of any single case, we have but to make it our own. The parent has but to think of the child "once dead and alive again," or the wife saved from widowhood, of receiving back her husband; and in every instance of such deliverance, and every effort of successful humanity, what fountains are opened of gratitude and joy! Not that we imagine, that but for any awards, which we can adjudge, such generous efforts would not have been made. We have too much confidence in the impulses of that nature, which God has given us, and in the teachings of that religion, which the Son of God's love has brought us, to suppose, that without the bestowment of pecuniary bounty men will be wanting to their fellow-men in the hour of peril. God has touched the heart of His children to finer issues, and has set *that* within us, to answer to the calls of human suffering, which depends on no societies, or on what societies can bestow. To encourage, therefore, and reward; to quicken rather than awaken benevolence; and to provide efficient means, which an enlightened philanthropy may employ, is the chief purpose of our Society. For the extent to which this purpose has been accomplished, it becomes us gratefully to acknowledge the sovereign Arbiter, "with whom are the issues of life and death;" and to consecrate all our endeavors by our faith in Him, who, in a sense far surpassing that, in which even the most faithful of His disciples may hope to imitate Him, "came not to destroy men's lives but to save them." And amidst the calamities and crimes disordering society, which the lover of his race is so often called to contemplate and deplore, it is grateful to turn our thoughts to those heroic deeds, such as we here exhibit, which may at once restore our confidence in the nature, of which we are all partakers, and reveal to us the power of that religious faith, which is the only unfailing source of generous action.

OFFICERS AND TRUSTEES

OF

THE HUMANE SOCIETY,

FOR 1876-7.

LIST OF OFFICERS OF THE SOCIETY.

FROM ITS FORMATION TO THE PRESENT TIME.

PRESIDENTS.

JAMES BOWDOIN,
THOMAS RUSSELL,
JONATHAN MASON,
JOHN WARREN,
AARON DEXTER,
WILLIAM SPOONER,
JONATHAN AMORY,
BENJAMIN RICH,
FRANCIS PARKMAN,
DAVID SEARS,
F. B. CROWNINSHIELD.

FIRST VICE PRESIDENTS.

THOMAS RUSSELL,
JONATHAN MASON,
JOHN WARREN,
SIMEON HOWARD,
JOHN LATHROP,
THOMAS DAWES,
WILLIAM SPOONER,
SAMUEL COBB,
BENJAMIN RICH,
JOHN C. WARREN,
CHARLES LOWELL,
FRANCIS PARKMAN,
ROBERT G. SHAW,
JOHN HOMANS,
ROBERT B. FORBES.

SECOND VICE PRESIDENTS.

JOHN WARREN,
SIMEON HOWARD,
JOHN LATHROP,
AARON DEXTER,
WILLIAM SPOONER,
SAMUEL PARKMAN,
SAMUEL COBB,
JONATHAN AMORY,
JOHN C. WARREN,
CHARLES LOWELL,
FRANCIS PARKMAN,
ROBERT G. SHAW,
DANIEL P. PARKER,
ABBOTT LAWRENCE,
WILLIAM APPLETON,
SAMUEL HOOPER,
ROBERT B. FORBES,
SAMUEL K. LOTHROP.

TREASURERS.

SIMEON HOWARD,
SAMUEL PARKER,
EDWARD GRAY,
JOHN ELIOT,
SAMUEL COBB,
EPHRAIM ELIOT,
HENDERSON INCHES,
JOHN L. GARDNER,
CHARLES AMORY,
F. B. CROWNINSHIELD,
JOSEPH P. GARDNER,
CALEB A. CURTIS.

CORRESPONDING SECRETARIES.

THOMAS WELSH,
JOHN CLARKE,
SAMUEL PARKER,
AARON DEXTER,
WILLIAM SPOONER,
GEORGE G. LEE,
CHARLES LOWELL,
JOHN HEARD, Jr.
JACOB BIGELOW,
JOHN HOMANS,
SAMUEL K. LOTHROP,
CHARLES D. HOMANS.

RECORDING SECRETARIES.

JOHN CLARKE,
SAMUEL PARKER,
JOHN AVERY, Jr.
EDWARD GRAY,
CHARLES DAVIS,
FRANCIS J. OLIVER,
FRANCIS PARKMAN,
SAMUEL A. ELIOT,
JOHN L. GARDNER,
SAMUEL HOOPER,
HENRY A. PEIRCE,
JOHN P. BAYLEY,
AUGUSTUS T. PERKINS.

TRUSTEES.

SAMUEL PARKER,
JOHN LATHROP,
AARON DEXTER,
OLIVER WENDELL,
SAMUEL STILLMAN,
NATHANIEL BALCH,
SAMUEL HENSHAW,
PETER THACHER,
THOMAS WELSH,
JOHN AVERY, Jr.
JOHN CLARKE,
JEREMIAH ALLEN,
WILLIAM SPOONER,
SAMUEL PARKMAN,
JAMES SCOTT,
EDWARD GRAY,
WILLIAM PHILLIPS,
JOSEPH COOLIDGE,
WILLIAM EMERSON,
SAMUEL BRADFORD,
JONATHAN CHAPMAN,
BENJAMIN RICH,
JOSEPH S. BUCKMINSTER,
THOMAS DAWES,
CHARLES LOWELL,
GEORGE G. LEE,
EPHRAIM ELIOT,
JONATHAN AMORY,
HENDERSON INCHES,
ANDREW RITCHIE,
JOHN C. WARREN,
BRYANT P. TILDEN,
SAMUEL COBB,
JOHN HEARD, Jr.
PETER O. THACHER,
FRANCIS PARKMAN,
JOSEPH COOLIDGE,
ROBERT G. SHAW,
DANIEL P. PARKER,
JOHN GORHAM,
GEORGE HAYWARD,
EDWARD H. ROBBINS,
JACOB BIGELOW,
JOHN C. GRAY,
SAMUEL A. ELIOT,
CHARLES P. CURTIS,
JONATHAN M. WAINWRIGHT,
JOHN L. GARDNER,
JOHN HOMANS,
HENRY OXNARD,
ABBOTT LAWRENCE,
WILLIAM APPLETON,
CHARLES G. LORING,
ROBERT B. FORBES,
SAMUEL HOOPER,
DAVID SEARS,
SAMUEL AUSTIN,
CHARLES AMORY,
FRANCIS B. CROWNINSHIELD,
SAMUEL K. LOTHROP,
J. MASON WARREN,
FRANCIS BACON,
GEORGE B. UPTON,
WILLIAM AMORY,
HENRY A. PEIRCE,
JAMES DAVIS,
HENRY P. STURGIS,
DAVID SEARS, Jr.
JOHN P. BAYLEY,
NATHANIEL THAYER,
JOSEPH P. GARDNER,
CHARLES D. HOMANS,
JOHN HEARD,
AUGUSTUS T. PERKINS,
HENRY A. WHITNEY,
CALEB A. CURTIS,
H. HOLLIS HUNNEWELL.

LIST OF GENTLEMEN WHO HAVE DELIVERED DISCOURSES BEFORE THE HUMANE SOCIETY SINCE ITS INSTITUTION.

1787	JOHN LATHROP, D. D.
1788	SIMEON HOWARD, D. D.
1789	PETER THACHER, D. D.
1790	BENJAMIN WATERHOUSE, M. D.
1791	SAMUEL PARKER, D. D.
1792	JOHN BARTLETT, M. D.
1793	JOHN CLARK, D. D.
1794	THOMAS BARNARD, D. D.
1795	HON. JOHN BROOKS.
1796	CHANDLER ROBBINS, D. D.
1797	JOHN FLEET, M. D.
1798	WILLIAM WALTER, D. D.
1799	ISAAC HURD, M. D.
1800	REV. THOMAS THACHER.
1801	JEDIDIAH MORSE, D. D.
1802	ELIPHALET PORTER, D. D.
1803	JOHN S. J. GARDNER, D. D.
1804	JOHN HOWARD, M. D.
1805	THOMAS GRAY, D. D.
1806	THADDEUS M. HARRIS, D. D.
1807	REV. WILLIAM EMERSON.
1808	THOMAS DANFORTH, M. D.
1809	JOSEPH M'KEAN, LL. D.
1810	JOHN T. KIRKLAND, D. D.
1811	LEMUEL SHAW, LL. D.
1812	REV. HENRY COLMAN.
1813	JAMES KENDALL, D. D.
1814	JOHN ALLYN, D. D.
1815	REV. HORACE HOLLEY.
1816	JOHN GORHAM, M. D.
1817	WILLIAM TUDOR, ESQ.*

* At a special meeting of the Society, March, 1818, it was voted, partly in consideration of the increasing number of charitable occasions, to discontinue the public celebrations. Most of the preceding discourses were published.

ACT OF INCORPORATION.

Commonwealth of Massachusetts.

IN THE YEAR OF OUR LORD ONE THOUSAND SEVEN HUNDRED AND NINETY-ONE.

AN ACT

To Incorporate and Establish a Society by the name of The Humane Society of the Commonwealth of Massachusetts.

WHEREAS, it is the duty of government at all times to countenance and support its citizens in their exertions for alleviating the distresses of their fellow-men ; and whereas, divers persons have petitioned this Court for an act of incorporation whereby they may more effectually carry into execution their benevolent designs : —

Be it therefore enacted by the Senate and House of Representatives in General Court assembled, and by the authority of the same, That the Hon. Thomas Russell, Esq., Jonathan Mason, Esq., John Warren, M. D., Rev. Simeon Howard, D. D., Rev. Samuel Parker, D. D., John Avery, Jun. Esq., Rev. John Lathrop, D. D., Rev. Peter Thacher, Rev. John Clarke, Dr. Thomas Welsh, Aaron Dexter, M. D., and Mr. Nathaniel Balch, together with all those who now are, and such others who shall become members thereof, be, and they are hereby erected into and made a body politic corporate forever, by the name of The Humane Society of the Commonwealth of Massachusetts.

And be it further enacted by the authority aforesaid, That the said Corporation are hereby declared, and made capable in law of having, holding, purchasing, and taking in fee simple, or any less estate, by gift, grant, devise, or otherwise, any lands, tenements, or other estate, real and personal; provided that the annual income of the said real and personal estate shall not exceed the sum of four thousand pounds; and also to sell, alien, devise, or dispose of the same estate, real and personal, not using the same in trade or commerce.

And be it further enacted by the authority aforesaid, That the said Corporation shall have full power and authority to make, have, and use a common seal, and the same to break, alter, and renew at pleasure; that it shall be capable in law to sue and be sued, plead and be impleaded, answer and be answered unto, defend and be defended in all courts of record, or other courts or places whatsoever, in all actions, real, personal, and mixed, and to do and execute all and singular other matters and things, that to them shall and may appertain to do.

And be it further enacted by the authority aforesaid, That the said Corporation may make, establish, and put in execution such laws and regulations as may be necessary to the government of said Corporation; provided the same shall in no case be repugnant to the laws and constitution of this State; and for the well governing of the said Corporation, and the ordering of their affairs, they shall have such officers as they shall hereafter from time to time elect and appoint; and such officers as shall be designated by the laws and regulations of the said Corporation for the purpose, shall be capable of exercising such power for the well governing and ordering the affairs of the said Corporation, and calling and holding such occasional meetings for that purpose, as shall be fixed and determined by the said laws and regulations.

And be it further enacted by the authority aforesaid, That the end and design of the institution of the said Society, is for the recovery of persons who meet with such accidents as produce in them the appearance of death, and for promoting the cause of humanity by pursuing such means from time to time, as shall have for their object the preservation of human life, and the alleviation of its miseries.

And be it further enacted, That the place where the first meeting of the said Society shall be held, shall be in the town of Boston; and that the Hon. Thomas Russell, Esq., be, and he hereby is, authorized and empowered to fix the time for holding the said meeting, and to notify the same to the members of the said Society, by causing the same to be published in one of the Boston newspapers fourteen days before the time fixed on for holding the said meeting.

In the House of Representatives, Feb. 21, 1791.

This Bill having had three several readings, passed to be enacted.

DAVID COBB, *Speaker.*

In Senate, Feb. 23, 1791.

This Bill having had two several readings, passed to be enacted.

SAMUEL PHILLIPS, *President.*

By the Governor approved.

JOHN HANCOCK.

True copy. Attest,

JOHN AVERY, JUN., *Secretary.*

GENERAL STATUTES OF MASSACHUSETTS.

Chapter 161, Section 88.

OF OFFENCES AGAINST PROPERTY.

(Injury or removal, etc., to property of Humane Society.)

Whoever unlawfully enters any house or hut, the property of the Humane Society, and wilfully injures, destroys, removes, or carries away any food, fuel, oil, candles, furniture, utensils, or other property belonging to said Society, or unlawfully or wilfully enters any boat-house of said Society, and carries away, removes, or injures, any life-boat, car, or any of the ropes, tackle, oars, or any appurtenance thereof, or wilfully injures, or destroys, or unlawfully uses or commits any trespass upon the property of said Society, intended or kept for the purpose of saving or preserving human life, or commits any trespass upon such hut or boat-house, shall be punished by a fine not exceeding one hundred dollars, or by imprisonment in the jail not exceeding ninety days; but the penalties of this section shall not apply to persons for whose use said boats, houses, and other property are intended and kept. Pilots, commissioners of wrecks, sheriffs and their deputies, and constables, shall make complaint against all persons guilty of any offence under this section.

BY-LAWS.

ARTICLE I.

The officers of the Humane Society of the Commonwealth of Massachusetts shall consist of twelve Trustees, of whom one shall be President, two Vice-Presidents, one Treasurer, one Recording Secretary and one Corresponding Secretary. There shall also be annually appointed, from the Board of Trustees, a Standing Committee of three, a Finance Committee of two, and an Auditing Committee of two.

ARTICLE II.

The President, Vice-Presidents, Treasurer, Recording Secretary, Corresponding Secretary, and Trustees, shall be elected by ballot at the Annual Meeting, and shall hold their offices until others are chosen in their stead. In case of the death, absence or inability to act, of any officer, his duties shall devolve as follows, to wit: In case of the President, his duties shall devolve upon the first Vice-President; in case of the first Vice-President, upon the second Vice-President; in case of the Treasurer, upon the Recording Secretary; in case of the Recording Secretary, upon the Corresponding Secretary; and in case of the disability of both Treasurer and Recording Secretary, the duties of Treasurer shall devolve upon the Corresponding Secretary.

ARTICLE III.

The Trustees, a major part of whom shall constitute a quorum, shall have the entire care and management of all the concerns and funds of the Society, and may fill any vacancy in their board or in the offices of the Society. They shall also adjudge such rewards of merit as they may see fit, agreeably to the Charter and the By-Laws of the Society. Upon the resignation of any Trustee, his membership in the Society shall continue without further personal service, all persons chosen Trustees, thereby becoming members of the Society.

ARTICLE IV.

The Treasurer shall be in duty bound to see that all property belonging to the Society is held in its corporate name, and all evidences of said property shall remain in his custody. He shall have power to collect all dividends and other dues to the Society, and all transfers of stocks and other property of the Society shall be signed by the Treasurer and approved by one or more of the Finance Committee, which approval shall be in writing on the transfer signed by them. The Treasurer shall, with the approval of the Finance Committee, make all investments of the funds of the Society, and charge the same from time to time. The Treasurer shall also at the Annual Meeting, and at such other times as he may be requested so to do, by the Trustees, make a full exhibit of the accounts of the Society, which shall be examined and approved by the Auditing Committee at least once in every year. No money shall be paid by the Treasurer, without a vote of the Trustees or an order from the President, or on account of bills duly approved by the chairman of the Standing Committee.

ARTICLE V.

The Recording Secretary shall record all the votes of the Society, and shall keep an abstract of its proceedings, and shall record in full all such communications as the Trustees shall direct, and shall call the meetings of the Society and of the Trustees.

ARTICLE VI.

The Corresponding Secretary shall perform all the correspondence of the Society, reporting the same for the approval of the Trustees.

ARTICLE VII.

The Standing Committee shall have the general charge and detail of all the Huts, Boats, and Life-Saving apparatus of every kind, belonging to the Society, and shall make a written report, to be presented at the meeting of the Board.

ARTICLE VIII.

The Annual Meeting of the Society shall be holden on the second Tuesday in April, at which time it may elect members by a two-thirds vote, and the President shall call special meetings either of the Society or of the Trustees, at the request of three of the Trustees.

ARTICLE IX.

Notice of all meetings of the Society shall be given by publishing the same in some daily morning newspaper in the city of Boston, not less than three times. The first publication to be seven days before, and the last on the day of the meeting.

ARTICLE X.

Meetings of the Trustees shall be held on the first Friday of every month, at such time and place as the Recording Secretary shall appoint, unless otherwise directed by the Trustees. Notices of such meetings shall be sent to them one week previous to such meeting, and if it be a special meeting, it shall be so stated in the notice.

ARTICLE XI.

Any person within this Commonwealth, or any citizen of this Commonwealth, who shall by signal exertion or peril save or attempt to save human life, or any person who shall by signal exertion or peril save or attempt to save the life of a citizen of this Commonwealth, may be entitled to receive a reward not exceeding twenty dollars in money, or either of the medals, or the certificate of the Society.

ARTICLE XII.

There shall be a common seal of the Society, and on it engraved a representation of the rescue of Moses by the daughter of Pharaoh, with the motto, I drew him from the waters. Exodus xi. 10.

ARTICLE XIII.

These By-Laws may at any time be amended, at any meeting of the Society called for that purpose.

PREMIUMS AWARDED BY THE TRUSTEES.

Of the large number of Premiums awarded for benevolent exertions, we select those chiefly which appear to be distinguished from the rest, by the merit and interest of the case, or the amount of the premium. The present list will be found, therefore, to include not more than a quarter part of the whole number, and, with few exceptions, are such as were thought worthy of some special consideration by the Trustees.*

The first List of Premiums which was published, was that appended to the discourse delivered before the Society, at its anniversary of June, 1792. It is thus introduced:

"The Trustees, with great pleasure, announce to the public the exertions of such of their fellow-citizens as have been instrumental in saving from death a number of persons, who must otherwise inevitably have perished. For such exertions, the following premiums have been adjudged."

1786. To Mr. Andrew Sloan, who by signal exertion saved a lad from drowning among the ice near the Mill Dam† in Boston, £0 28 0

* A large number of other cases will be found in the former publications of the Trustees, for which smaller sums were awarded, varying from one or two to ten dollars.

† The "Mill Dam," at the time of this record, was near what is now Causeway Street.

F

1787. To Mrs. MARY CAPELL, who, by persevering use of the methods recommended by the Society, resuscitated the child of a painter who fell into a deep cistern and was taken out apparently dead, £0 28 0

1789. To LIEUT. SCOTT, of His Most Christian Majesty's Ship, the Leopard, for risking his life, in jumping from the stern of said ship, then in the harbor of Boston, and saving the life of a young lad,—A GOLD MEDAL, £2 12 0

1790. To Mr. GOFFE, for receiving into his house, for the purpose of using the means of resuscitation, the body of Mr. Davis, who fell from the stern of a ship, at Governor's Wharf, when this act of kindness was refused at Mr. Davis's own lodgings,—the thanks of the Society, and a Premium of £3 0 0

1791. To M. JULIEN JEAN DUROTOER, for saving the lives of Daniel Pierce and three other men, who were shipwrecked near Nantucket Shoals, in December last, £3 0 0

1792. To JOHN and THOMAS BURGESS, keepers of the light-house at the Gurnet, for their exertions in saving the lives of two of the unfortunate crew of the ship Columbia, wrecked on Duxbury Beach, £3 0 0

To Mr. RICHARD HALL, on representation of Rev. Dr. Osgood, of Medford, for saving the life of a young student, in Mr. Woodbridge's Academy, a SILVER MEDAL, with suitable inscriptions, to be presented by the President of the Society.

1793. To S. DELANO, Jr., for saving the crew of the ship Rodney, wrecked on Duxbury Beach, a MEDAL OF GOLD, valued at £4 12 4

To R. HALL, Jr., for saving a boy, a MEDAL OF SILVER, value, £1 13 0

To P. GEYER and others, for saving the lives of several persons, wrecked on Long Island, £2 8 0

To the Rev. Mr. Shaw, and Mr. Elisha Doane, five guineas, to be by them distributed among those benevolent persons, inhabitants of Cohasset, who exerted themselves in saving Capt. Hans, Peter Klein, and the crew of the ship Gertrude Maria, of Copenhagen, when in imminent peril of death.

1794. To J. WHITNEY and L. MORSE, for saving a man from drowning, $10

To S. SMITH, 60s., and H. BREDLEE, 30s., for saving a man, $15

To W. WHITE, for saving a woman, $5

To DOLPHIN GALLER, for saving the life of a child of Mr. George Churchill, of Plymouth, $10

To JOHN HOWELL, GEORGE DUNTON, and JOHN BROWN, for saving the life of a son of Mr. Parker, who had fallen through the ice in the Mill Creek, $17

1795. To ROBERT ROGERS, for saving the lives of four boys, overset in a boat where the water was seven feet deep, $5

To NATHANIEL TRENCH and SON, for saving the lives of Henry Emmes, John Emmes, J. Snelling, and William Harris, who were overset in a small boat in the harbor of Boston, and would have perished but for the said Trench, $8

1796. To TIMOTHY PIKE and JOSEPH BARRETT, for resuscitating a person of seventy years of age, who had fallen into the water in passing over the causeway, $5

To PATRICK MORGAN, for bringing on shore the body of a child of Henry Rogers, of Springfield, $5

To EBENEZER ADAMS and LORAINE FENNO, for saving the life of Peter Munwell, between Spectacle and Thompson's Islands, $10

To SAMUEL POLLY, for saving Benjamin Buckman, who was overset in a gale of wind upon Chelsea shore, $10

To JACOB WHIPPLE, for saving Andrew Magee, William Penniman, and his daughter, who were overset in a sudden gust of wind, $10

1797. To WILLIAM HANCOCK and SAMUEL BUNTING, for attempting to save the life of Mr. Tileston, who was suffocated in a well upon the Boston Pier, ten dollars each, $20

To JONATHAN COOPER, for bringing up said Tileston, Hancock, and Bunting, who were also suffocated in their attempt to save Tileston, $10, and a SILVER MEDAL, value, $4, $14

To ADAM SMITH, for saving two children at Hancock's Wharf, $8

To SILAS LIBBEY, for taking up a son of Major Hasty, of Scarborough, $10

To MAJOR LIBBEY, for his uncommon despatch in procuring a Physician for the above case, a SILVER MEDAL, $6

To WILSON ADLINGTON, for saving the life of Francis Whiston, $6

1798. To JOSHUA HARDY and GEORGE REX, for saving a child of Edmund Steven, four dollars each, $8

To SAMUEL COX, Jr., for saving John Thompson, $10

To JOHN HEBDEN and EBENEZER WARD, for their exertions in saving the life of Ralph Riddle, $10

To Mr. JOHN LOW, on representation of Mrs. Catharine Annesly, who was a spectator of the act, for descending into a well, and rescuing thence a child, $4

To Mr. SAMUEL COX, on representation of Shubael Bell, Esq., for perilous efforts in saving John Thomas, upset in a boat, $10

And to the MAN, who lives on Governor's Island, for receiving and relieving the same, $4

1799. To Mr. JONATHAN LORING, for signal exertions in saving the life of a child, as testified by several respectable persons, $8

To Mr. A. CLAPP, for going into the water with his clothes on, and exertions in saving a child, $8

To a young lad, by the name of PETER MOODY, for saving two persons from drowning, $10

1800. To ISAAC WHEELER, for saving the life of Allen Nickerson, when in much peril, $10

To CAPT. GEORGE CROWNINSHIELD, on representation of Rev. William Bentley, of Salem, for special exertions in saving a youth in imminent peril, a handsome GOLD MEDAL, with a suitable inscription, $20

1801. To CAPT. JAMES PERKINS, Sen., and JAMES PERKINS, Jr., of Arundel, Me., Two SILVER CANS, as an honorable testimony from the Trustees, for their signal exertions in saving the lives of six persons, when in the utmost danger,* $60

* At a meeting of the Trustees, October 6, 1801, on a communication from the Hon. Daniel Dewey, representing the extraordinary exertions of Mr. Joseph North, of Augusta, Maine, in saving the life of Mr. Amos Bond, from drowning, a gold medal was voted to Mr. North, and silver medals to each of two other individuals who assisted him. The inscription on the former of which, as directed by a committee appointed for the purpose, was as follows:

PRESENTED
BY THE
Humane Society of Massachusetts,
TO
MR. JOSEPH NORTH, JUN.,
WHO, WITH A SOUL SUPERIOR
TO ALL CONSIDERATIONS OF PERSONAL
SAFETY, PRESERVED THE LIFE OF
MR. AMOS BOND,
WHEN DROWNING IN A RAPID AND MERCILESS
CURRENT NEAR KENNEBECK BRIDGE,
IN AUGUSTA, APRIL 17, 1801.
ALSO THE LIFE OF
WILLIAM PITT,
NEAR THE SAME PLACE,
AUGUST, 1798.

1802. To EPHRAIM COLVER, of Chesterfield, for saving the life of a young man in Westfield River, $10

To ADAM WALLACE THAXTER, for saving the life of a child, $5

To GEORGE JOHNSON, of Salem, for saving the life of Virgil Maxey, $10

To Mr. PARSONS, for receiving into his house the body of Quaco, a Negro, (who was drowned at the bottom of the Common,) for the purpose of using the resuscitative process, $5

1803. To NEHEMIAH JEQUITH, aged 76, for saving the life of John Danley, of Tyngsborough, who had fallen through the ice in Merrimack River, $10

To JOSIAH BATES, DAVID COLE, and EBEN COLE, for saving the life of Levi Gifford, at sea, $9

To ASA PETTENGILL, of Methuen, for saving the lives of several persons near Bodwell's Falls, $30

To HENRY BRAGDON, for saving the life of Mr. Hatch, who fell from a small float in York River, $8

To NATHANIEL DAVIS, for saving the life of Hugh Ramsey, in Mystic River, $10

To GRIFFIN BARNES, for his signal exertions in saving the life of a child of Mr. Norcross, a GOLD MEDAL, $8 94

1804. To JOHN BARNES, for saving the life of Ephraim Davis, a MEDAL, $9 89

To EPHRAIM HOSKINS, for saving the life of a son of Mrs. Farmer, Plymouth, $10

To ISAAC B. RICH and JOSHUA SMITH, for saving the life of a man who fell into the Dock near Bray's Wharf, $12

To MOSES WADSWORTH, for attempting to save the life of J. Jackson, who fell through the ice in a pond at Medfield, $10

To PAUL DAVIS, for saving the life of Jonas Twiss, who fell through the ice near Prison Point, $10

To ELISHA ABBOTT, for saving two children who fell from a wharf near Charlestown Bridge, $10

To OLIVER JORDAN, for his signal exertions in saving a young lad from drowning, $5

To Mr. BRAY COX, $10, and to the other persons with him, being thirteen in number, $5 each, for their humane exertions in saving three men and a woman, as stated in Rev. Mr. Alden's letter,* $75

To GEORGE SAMPSON, Jr., for signal exertions in saving the child, mentioned in Dr. Thacher's letter,* $10

To the Rev. TIMOTHY ALDEN, of Portsmouth, for the use of Mr. BENNING HALL, for his signal exertions in saving the life of a young lad, named John Hart, from drowning, $10

1805. To ANTHONY GOWEN and PETER BRETTON, for their exertions in saving the life of a son of Rev. Dr. Eckley from drowning, and for bringing up the dead body of the drowned seaman, who was with him, five dollars each, $10

To the OWNER OF THE HOUSE, who received the dead body of said seaman, $5

To Mr. WILLIAM LEONARD, and the other persons of Plymouth, who preserved the captain and seamen of ship Hibernia, when shipwrecked, as mentioned in the letter of Dr. James Thacher, $50

To JOSEPH PRESTON and JOSEPH CHASE, for their exertions in saving the life of one John Green, $10

To JACOB and PETER LONG, for taking from the water a new-born mulatto child, $4

* The letters of Dr. Thacher, of Plymouth, and of Rev. T. Alden, of Portsmouth, exhibiting highly interesting cases, appear in the appendix to Dr. Howard's and Dr. Gray's anniversary discourses, 1804–5.

To WILLIAM POWER, commander of the schooner Eleanor; to ARCHIBALD ST. DENNIS, commander of the schooner Plough-Boy; and to JOHN POWER, commander of the Minerva, for their signal exertions in rescuing and receiving on board their respective vessels the passengers of the ship Jupiter, foundered at sea, — a SILVER CAN, each, with suitable inscriptions, emblematical of the event, the value not to exceed the sum of thirty dollars each, together with the thanks of the Trustees to the crews of their respective vessels, $90

1806. To BENJAMIN PAGE, of Quincy, for signal exertions in saving a son of N. Curtis, $10

To SAMUEL JONES, for saving a child of Mr. George Singleton, who had fallen into a well of thirty feet in depth, when there were about twelve feet of water therein. $10

To EBENEZER ROWE and SHUBAEL SELLEY, on recommendation of Rev. Alden Bradford, of Wiscasset, twenty dollars, each, for their humane and gallant exertions in saving Joseph Boynton and James Handley, together with the thanks of the Trustees, $40

Also, to the same, for their perilous, though unsuccessful efforts to rescue Master Coffin, five dollars each, $10

To BARKER BRYANT, and his assistants, for taking from a fishing-boat, Abigail Brown, when in imminent danger of drowning, $16

To BENJAMIN TARBELL, for signal exertions in saving a child that fell into a well at Castle William, measuring ninety feet deep, $10

1807. To JOEL PHILLEBROOK and JAMES FULLER, for saving Capt. Thomas Chase, and twelve others, from the wreck of the schooner Welcome Return, when in imminent danger of perishing on a desolate coast, thirty dollars each, $60

To ICHABOD HALL and SYLVANUS STURTEVANT, for humane exertions in saving, the one an adult, the other a young child, the cases being stated by James Thacher, M. D., Plymouth, $10

1808. To JESSE B. WILCOX, for saving Richard Day, in a very perilous condition, as stated by Rev. Dr. Gardiner, a spectator of the transaction, and assisting in the same, $10

To L. STEPHENSON, of Cohasset, for his great exertions in preserving Mrs. Snow from drowning; and his laudable, though unsuccessful, exertions in endeavoring to save the three children of Mr. Snow, a GOLD MEDAL, of $10

Also, to NEWCOMB BATES and four others, for aiding in the same, a GOLD MEDAL, of the value of $5 to each, $25

To HOLBROOK and JORDAN, for saving several who were overset in a boat on Dorchester Flats, $10

To JOSIAH LAMBORD, JOSEPH RICH, and four others, all of Truro, for saving a number of people left upon the wreck of the schooner Active, of Harpswell, which foundered October 28, near Cape Cod Lighthouse, six dollars each, $36

1809. To Messrs. WHITE, MORE, and GURNEY, ten dollars each, for their exertions in saving two men belonging to Fort Independence, who in a violent snow-storm had fallen through the ice, in crossing from South Boston, $30

To BILL, a native of the Sandwich Islands, for jumping into the water, ("paying no regard thereto, being perfectly used to it in his own country,") and rescuing a man who had fallen in, and could not swim, $5

1810. To SHELDON HOBBS, a youth of fifteen years, for rescuing two children of Berwick, Maine, who had fallen under the ice while skating, a GOLD MEDAL, $10

To Mr. SILAS HATHAWAY and his son FREDERICK, the thanks of the Trustees, and a premium of ten dollars, for their very laudable exertions in saving the life of young David B. Harvey, of Plymouth, $10

1811. To LEVI STODDARD, for taking up Capt. Stairs from a wreck, when in a perilous condition, $10

To JOHN ALLEN, Jr., on recommendation of Dr. James Thacher, of Plymouth, for his heroic exertions in saving the life of the son of Mr. John Patee, a GOLD MEDAL, $10

1812. To CALEB HOPKINS RAND, a lad of fourteen, for plunging into a cistern and rescuing his brother, who when taken out was apparently dead, a GOLD MEDAL, $10

N. B. It appeared in this case to the Trustees, that a man who was near to the cistern at the time of the accident, thought the danger so great, that, although earnestly solicited, he refused any assistance.

To SAMUEL BANNISTER, for saving the life of a lad, who was drowning on the north side of Long Wharf, the Society's GOLD MEDAL, $10

To CHARLES WILLARD, a minor, for saving the life of George Baker, $10

1813. To ROMANUS EMERSON, CHARLES HARRINGTON, and six others, for great exertions and considerable expense in saving a soldier caught in the ice in a boat, when deserting from Governor's Island, $50

To JOHN FARRINGTON, for heroic exertions in saving the life of John Cotton, of Malden, who fell through the ice in attempting to cross Mystic River, $10

And to Mrs. FARRINGTON, for her kindness when Mr. Cotton was brought to her house, $2

To Mr. ELLIS BARTLETT, for great and signal exertions in saving Capt. Wendell Churchill, whose schooner was cast on shore, near Plymouth Harbor, the case being recommended by Dr. James Thacher, $10

To CAPT. WILLIAM MARTIN, Master of the brig Iris, for generous and persevering exertions in saving the life of Capt. John Howe, in the harbor of St. Ubes, the Society's GOLD MEDAL,* $10

To JOHN PALMER, for saving the life of Green Sears, by signal and persevering exertions, the Society's GOLD MEDAL, or $10

1814. To WILLIAM SAVAGE, of Boston, for heroic exertions in saving two children, when in great danger of drowning, the Society's GOLD MEDAL, of value $10

To JOHN DUNN, for saving the life of John Baxter, $10

To THOMAS CARTER, of Newburyport, for saving his class-mate, Joseph Coolidge, while bathing in Charles River, at Cambridge, June 8th, the Society's GOLD MEDAL, and that the Corresponding Secretary present to him the same, $10

To N. NASH, for saving a son of Lewis Leland, $10

To JACOB ROBINSON, for his exertions in saving the life of Benjamin Foster, on the 17th June last, a GOLD MEDAL, or $10

To JOHN R. MOORE, for persevering exertions in saving the life of a little girl, on Sunday, September 18th, $10

1815. To WILLIAM BRINTNELL, for his humane attentions and exertions in receiving into his house the captain, crew and passengers of the sloop Mason's Daughter, eight in number, after she was wrecked on a rock, in Broad Sound, near one of the Brewster Islands, $10

To ISAAC MERRILL, for exertions in saving the lives of two men, at Amoskeag Falls, the Society's GOLD MEDAL; or, at his option, $10

* Dr. LATHROP, in presenting this case, mentioned in detail some circumstances attending the preservation of Capt. Howe, of which not the least remarkable was, that in dragging for him, one of the hooks of the drag inserted itself into his cheek, while another of the hooks caught in the ribband with which his hair was tied, held fast, and was the means of saving him.

And to JOSIAH GILLIS and ISRAEL HARDY, for assisting in the same, five dollars each, $10

To Mr. LAWRENCE NICHOLS, for his very extraordinary exertions and well-directed efforts in saving the lives of Messrs. Isaac Rouse and J. P. Richardson, when in imminent danger, near Boston Light House, on the 16th of June last, a GOLD MEDAL, of the value of $30

To JOHN PETERSON, of Edgecomb, Maine, and to JOSIAH FRITH, of Wiscasset, for saving the lives of John Cochran and Allen Malcomb, a GOLD MEDAL, or ten dollars each, $20

To JOHN SEVEY, for humane efforts in saving Joseph Roby, of Wiscasset, the Society's GOLD MEDAL, $10

To JOHN NICHOLSON, of Plymouth, for saving the life of a son of Mr. Ansel Robbins, a SILVER MEDAL, of the value of $5

To HENRY DOANE, GEORGE HALL, OBADIAH LINCOLN, and LEVI OAKES, all of Cohasset, for their skill, perseverance, and heroism, in saving the lives of two men from the wreck of the schooner Armistice, of Portland, thrown on Cohasset Rocks by the great storm of the 31st of August last, the Society's GOLD Medal, each, with suitable inscriptions thereon, $40

To JOHN WOOD, for extraordinary exertions in saving a little boy, of four years old, when in great danger of drowning in the Mill Creek, $10

1816. To ALEXANDER MITCHELL, and four others, for their hazardous, persevering, and laudable exertions in attempting to save the lives of two sons of Mr. A. Harlow, of Cambridge, and of Mr. Kimball, GOLD MEDALS of ten dollars each, $50

To BENJAMIN RICE, and his young brother, WILLIAM, "for extraordinary and hazardous exertions in rescuing Mrs. Whitefield and her grandson, a boy of about seven years of age, both of whom, in attempting to cross Accossnet River, between

New Bedford and Fair Haven, had fallen under the ice, and for a considerable time were in the utmost peril, from which they were delivered by these two boys, in the presence of a number of men, whose efforts were paralyzed by fear, a SILVER MEDAL, of five dollars each, with fifteen dollars in money to the elder, and five dollars in money to the younger, and the thanks of the Trustees for their noble exertions," $30

To SHEPHERD BLANCHARD, for saving a child at Commercial Wharf, 20th July last, $10

And to JOHN KIMBALL, for rescuing from imminent danger of drowning, Francis Abbot, the same day, $10

To BRADDOCK LORING, for his laudable, though fruitless endeavors to save the life of a child, $10

To MILTON MOORE, of Russell, on representation of Hon. Justin Ely, for "bringing to the shore, at the peril of his own life, the body of Asa Adams, of Weston, who had sunk to the bottom of a pond in West Springfield, and was senseless, but, by great exertions, restored to health," $15

To SAMUEL WILLIAMS, of Augusta, Maine, on representation of Samuel Howard, Esq., for saving the life of Frederick Lithgow, who had sunk to the bottom of Kennebeck River, and was taken up senseless, but afterwards resuscitated, a GOLD MEDAL, with suitable inscriptions, to the value of $15

1817. To LIEUTENANT SALTER, of the United States Navy, for his intrepid and persevering exertions in saving, at the great hazard of his own life, the lives of two women and one man, in Boston Harbor, the Society's GOLD MEDAL, with suitable inscriptions, $10

To MIDSHIPMAN JOHN F. HOWELL, to MIDSHIPMAN GEORGE D. DODDS, and to Mr. JOHN MCCLOUD, Boatswain, of the ship Independence, a SILVER MEDAL, each, with suitable inscriptions.

The particulars of this interesting case, with the correspondence between the President of the Society and the commanding officer of the Independence, are detailed at length in the Records of the Trustees. A brief account is exhibited in the note below, taken from the Columbian Centinel of that date.*

* "On one of the remarkable cold days of last February, the following occurrence happened, the publication of which must be highly gratifying to the friends of humanity.

"On the morning of the 4th of February, two women embarked in a small boat, with only one boatman, to go on board the United States ship Independence, to which their husbands belong. There was much ice in the harbor, and the boat was driven by it from her course to the mouth of Medford river. Many persons standing on the wharves, saw the unhappy situation of these people with those distressing and painful emotions arising from a view of fellow-beings perishing, and the deprivation of the power of even attempting their rescue. They were considered lost by those on shore. LIEUT. WILLIAM FINCH, then commanding officer of the Independence, despatched a cutter with two midshipmen and a crew to their relief, furnishing such means as the ship afforded, to facilitate and effect it. After several unsuccessful attempts, and an interval of half an hour, the cutter returned with great difficulty, the men being nearly deprived, by the intense cold, of the power of exertion. LIEUT. FINCH, thinking it still possible to release and save the sufferers, appointed a fresh crew and ordered another attempt. LIEUT. WM. DAYTON SALTER asked permission to take charge of the cutter and direct the operations. The permission was given, and after great exertions and perseverance, he succeeded in getting within a short distance of the boat, and found the two women and man stretched at length and quite motionless. By the aid of planks, ropes, &c., LIEUT. SALTER, with his men, was enabled, with great hazard and difficulty, to take the poor sufferers from the boat on board the cutter, and covering them with blankets and jackets, kept them alive, and after two hours' labor in clearing themselves of the ice, arrived in safety on board the Independence. In the prosecution of this arduous and humane enterprise, LIEUT. SALTER was, more than once, in imminent danger of drowning, the plank giving way under his feet, and he and those with him suffered much from the frost. This conduct called forth the spontaneous admiration and applause of all on board the ship. Stout hearts were melted, and hard faces suffused with tears of joy. By kind and judicious attentions the rescued were eventually restored to health, and Mr. SALTER recovered the use of his feet and hands."

"Information of the above circumstances, and other facts connected with them, was communicated to the Trustees of the MASSACHUSETTS HUMANE SOCIETY, who, at a late meeting, voted that the thanks of the Society be presented to LIEUT. WILLIAM FINCH, for the promptness and judgment evinced by him, while commanding officer of the United States ship Independence, in giving such orders, and devising such measures as were, under the favor of Providence, the means of saving the lives of John Mannuel, Elizabeth Ireson, and Olive Brown, when in the most imminent danger in Boston Harbor, Feb. 4th, 1817."

To WILLIAM TEWKSBURY, of Deer Island, for the very extraordinary exertions by which four persons were saved on the 26th of May last, seventy dollars in money, and a SILVER MEDAL, of the value of ten dollars, $80

To his son, ABIJAH R., $35, and to his wife Elizabeth $20 for their efficient aid, $55

Also, to CHARLES STURGIS, for assistance on the same occasion, $5

1818. To ZACCHEUS WYMAN, of Utica, State of New York, for exertions in rescuing John P. Bigelow,* son of Hon. Timothy Bigelow, of Medford, from imminent danger of drowning in the Middlesex Canal, fifteen dollars in money, or a GOLD MEDAL, of that value, at his option, $15

To CAPTAIN WILLIAM ALLEN, of Plymouth, for uncommon exertions, as stated by Dr. James Thacher, in saving the lives of two lads, in Plymouth Harbor, 22d April last, $20

To JOTHAM and HENRY FULLER, for saving the life of Mr. Baldwin, of Fitchburg, in March last, ten dollars to the former, and five to the latter, $15

To JOSEPH BOLTON, of Biddeford, for extraordinary exertions in saving Daniel Brainerd, of Saco, when in great peril, $20

To THOMAS DOLLIVER, for rescuing John Barnes, Warren Alexander, and Henry Marston, when in peril of drowning, in the Light House Channel, $5

Also, to his son THOMAS, for assistance on the same occasion, a SILVER MEDAL.

1819. To Mr. JOHN WILSON, one of the Branch Pilots of Boston, for generous exertions in saving the lives of Capt. Nathaniel W. Merrill, and his men, when exposed to imminent peril, on the wreck of the "Susan and Sarah," December 6, 1818, a GOLD MEDAL, of the value of fifteen dollars, with

* The late Hon. John P. Bigelow, Mayor of Boston.

suitable inscriptions, and to his men, three in number, ten dollars each, $45

To WILLIAM WILTSHIRE, ESQ., Consul of His Britannic Majesty, at Mogadore, Morocco, for generous and disinterested exertions in rescuing Capt. Riley from slavery among the Arabs, the Society's GOLD MEDAL, with suitable inscriptions, $20

To CAPTAIN ELEAZER GRAVES, for rescuing a number of persons from a British brig which had been wrecked, and conveying them to Cowes ; also, for bringing home three American children, who were on board the brig, the Society's GOLD MEDAL, $20

1820. To EDMUND R. SMITH, and others, for saving seven men from perishing in the ice at South Boston, $45

To MOSES ROBINSON, and his two BROTHERS, of Waldoborough, Maine, for saving two men in Boston Harbor, five dollars each, $15

To Mr. HOLMES, in rescuing a number of United States soldiers from imminent danger of perishing in the ice, near South Boston, $10

And to others who assisted, together with the thanks of the Trustees for their efforts, $25

To MAJOR JOHN BARTLEMAN, of the British Royal Marines, for saving, at great personal peril, William O'Brien, a GOLD MEDAL, $20

To HORATIO SPRAGUE, ESQ., an American merchant, resident at Gibraltar, for his benevolence and patriotism, evinced in reimbursing William Wiltshire, Esq., British Consul at Mogadore, the money advanced by him in rescuing Capt. James Riley and his companions from slavery, the Society's GOLD MEDAL, with suitable inscriptions, and an honorary membership of the Society, $20

To WILLIAM TEWKSBURY, of Deer Island, in consideration of his many signal and perilous exertions in the cause of humanity, the sum of forty dollars, towards the purchase of a boat, $40

1821. To CYRUS RYE, of Maine, for rescuing four children, in danger of being drowned, $10

To JOHN BULFINCH, of Union, Maine, for rescuing Edward Foster, at great hazard, the Society's GOLD MEDAL, with inscriptions, $10

To JAMES P. KIDD, of the Independence, for saving, at the peril of his life, a young lad named Bassett, a GOLD MEDAL, with suitable inscriptions, $15

To WILLIAM H. FOWLE, and HENRY R. DEARBORN, two young gentlemen at Mr. Knapp's Academy, for rescuing, at the peril of their lives, Charles Rich,* son of Benjamin Rich, Esq., their fellow-student, when in imminent peril of drowning in a pond in Roxbury, the Society's GOLD MEDAL, with suitable inscriptions for each, $20

To JOHN LAKIN, a fisherman, for rescuing Capt. Eastman and a soldier of Fort Independence, when in peril, $10

To CORPORAL GEORGE MCAULY, WILLIAM MCGEE, and three others, stationed at the United States Fort, near Portsmouth, for rescuing the captain, crew, and passengers of the schooner President, of Thomaston, when wrecked on the Whale's Back, near Portsmouth, April 20th, the Society's SILVER MEDAL, of five dollars, and three dollars in money to each, $40

To HENRY WILLARD, of Roxbury, for heroic exertions in rescuing, at imminent hazard, the son of Mr. Elijah Mears, a GOLD MEDAL, $10

* Afterwards Rev. Charles Rich, of Nantucket.

To JONATHAN LAWRENCE, keeper of the Lighthouse, for rescuing three men when in danger of drowning, on the 16th of April last,* $10

1822. To HENRY ATWOOD, commander of the brig Draco, for his perseverance and humanity, whereby Captain William Fortune, and ten of his companions were saved from perishing on the wreck of a British brig, during a tempestuous night, January 5th, 1822, the Society's GOLD MEDAL, $20

Also, five dollars to each of his FOUR SEAMEN, who, at the risk of their lives, assisted, $20

To CAPTAIN JOHN SMITH, of the ship Hannah, of St. Johns, N. B., for relieving and saving the survivors of the crew of the brig Amsterdam, shipwrecked November, 1820, a GOLD MEDAL, $15

To CAPTAIN SIMEON NICKERSON, of the Phœbe, of Dennis, for judicious and humane exertions in rescuing from great peril Samuel Topliff and S. G. Lowe, when upset in a boat, the Society's GOLD MEDAL, twenty dollars, and to his son, assisting him, five dollars, $25

To RUFUS HAZARD, a colored person, for extraordinary exertions and great hazard, in attempting to save Samuel Williams, who had sunk in Squamcook River, $10

* That of the many applications made for rewards, some were found deceptive or groundless, will appear from the following extract from the records of this date, Sept. 3d, 1821. Other cases for like reasons were dismissed. "A certificate of the conduct of Daniel Geary, in rescuing John Carroll from danger of drowning in Reading Pond, in August last, *with a certificate of a Justice of the Peace for Middlesex County annexed*, was submitted for consideration; and the same having been investigated, it appeared that the leading facts of the case were as follows: Two young men and a boy were in a small boat, fishing in Reading Pond. The boy fell out of the boat in a fit, and probably would have been lost had those in the boat not assisted him. But having sunk once, and rising, he was taken into the boat again." From a view of the facts, the Trustees were unanimously of opinion, that no one was entitled to any reward whatever, it being an act only of common humanity, the refusing of which would have been disgraceful.

1823. To BENJAMIN SNOW, for saving Francis Marandi, when drowning near Sargent's Wharf, $10

To ROBERT PORTER, mate of the "Swift Messenger," for saving Miss Ryland, a passenger who had fallen from the vessel and must otherwise have drowned, $10

N. B. At the monthly meeting of the Trustees in August, 1823, premiums, varying in value from two to ten dollars, were awarded in *fourteen* different cases, one of which was to DANIEL WHITNEY, a boy of 13, for saving Ebenezer Morton, a boy of eleven years. The whole amount appropriated at this meeting was $82

1824. To LEVI GURNEY, HORACE WHITTEMORE, JAMES GORDON, and J. PORTER, for their exertions in saving from drowning a son of Mr. Nathaniel R. Sturgis, while skating on the Mill-dam basin, ten dollars each, or the Society's GOLD MEDAL, $40

To WILLIAM S. BRIDGE, for extraordinary efforts in saving the lives of two seamen, upset in a boat, a GOLD MEDAL, $10

And to L. NICKERSON and WILLIAM WHEATON, assisting, $15

To JAMES S. CUTTS, twenty dollars, to N. SHERMAN, ten dollars, and to HENRY GARDNER, five dollars, for perilous exertions in saving two boys of Salem, $35

To THOMAS WARD, for great judgment and presence of mind, in saving eleven persons, upset in Boston Harbor, June 14th, $20

N. B. At the monthly meeting in August, 1824, premiums varying from *one* dollar to *twenty*, upon *sixteen* distinct applications, were awarded, the whole amount bestowed being $121

Of these sixteen premiums, one of ten dollars was awarded to PAUL BAXTER, for saving the life of a son of Bradford Sumner,

Esq., who had fallen from a wharf into the water; another of twenty dollars, to GABRIEL MAHONY, who jumped from the brig Webster into the Atlantic, and saved L. P. Curtis; and a third, on the representation of Rev. Dr. Brazer, to NATHAN FISK, of Salem, and to two others, of Beverly, ten dollars each, for rescuing three men, in great danger of drowning; together with five dollars each, to two boys, THOMAS NEAT and THOMAS CLEMENS, assisting.

To WILLIAM PARKMAN, aged 13 years, for saving William H. Barnes, bathing near Hancock's Wharf, $10

To WILLIAM DOLE, of Newburyport, for signal exertions in saving Charles Defond, $10

To HENRY R. DEARBORN a SILVER CUP, and to FREDERICK DABNEY a SILVER MEDAL, for laudable efforts in rescuing Alexander F. A. Dunn, $20

1825. To NATHANIEL FRENCH, CALEB BEAL, and ELIJAH BEAL, for extraordinary exertions and great hazard, in rescuing Capt. Abraham Tower from a perilous situation, ten dollars each, or a CUP, $30

To JOHN SMITH, and his wife, MARY ANN, for rescuing Mrs. Jerusha Simonds, fallen from a bridge into a canal, near Lexington, $10

To ABIJAH R. and GEORGE TEWKSBURY, for hazardous exertions in saving the lives of John Gates and Benjamin Price, when in great peril, twenty dollars, or a MEDAL, each, $40

To Mrs. REBECCA WILSON, for successful exertions in rescuing two boys, Edward Howe and Horace Clarke, who had fallen from a wharf at Charlestown, $5

To HENRY PARKHURST, a lad about ten years old, for saving John Towers, $10

To RUFUS G. AMORY, Jr., for saving a lad, $8

1826. To G. W. SIMPSON, for rescuing Capt. Hill and his crew, $10

To SOLOMON HOPKINS, of Truro, for saving Josiah Cook, upset in a boat, in Barnstable Bay, $10

To BENJAMIN HODGKINS, for perilous efforts in rescuing Geo. R. Sargent and Wm. Freeman, $20

To JOHN S. PULSIFER, aged ten, for rescuing a son of Jonathan Mead, who had fallen from a wharf, $10

To TIMOTHY ALLEN, for saving five persons, upset in a boat, in Charlestown River, $20

And to his two men, assisting, five dollars each, $10

To CHARLES HARLOW, for saving a young child, $10

To WILLIAM P. MEAD, for rescuing two men, when in imminent danger in Quincy River, a Medal,* $10

1827. To JOHN C. KNOWLES and SON, of Eastham, and to COLONEL JOSEPH HOLBROOK, with two others, of Wellfleet, for spirited exertions in rescuing Capt. Josiah Trott and crew, when in imminent danger of drowning, off Cape Cod, ten dollars each, $50

To REUBEN COOMBS, mate of the Pilot-boat Leader, for rescuing Capt. Seth Adams, his crew and passengers, when in in imminent peril, near the Devil's Bank, a SILVER PITCHER, of the value of $50

Also, the thanks of the Trustees, to JOHN R. PARKER, ESQ., for communicating the danger to Mr. Coombs, by his telegraph.

To ASAPH GREENE, on representation of Col. Joseph May,

* At the meeting in December, Mr. Heard reported, that, upon diligent inquiry into several cases committed to him at the last meeting, he had reason to believe that the several persons represented to have been saved from drowning, had intentionally thrown themselves into the Mill Creek, for the purpose of obtaining the Society's premiums. That he had therefore refused to award any compensation for the services thus pretended to be rendered.

for rescuing from suffocation in a privy, a son of Charles C. Nichols,* $10

1828. To a daughter of Joseph Tufts, of Malden, for rescuing a son of Eben. Nichols, who had fallen into a well, the Society's certificate of thanks, together with $5

To JAMES STRATTON, who, in rescuing a boy in danger of drowning in the river, near Rev. Dr. Sharp's Church, had damaged his clothes and incurred a fit of sickness, $20

To WILLIAM G. BADGER and J. B. PORTER, on recommendation of N. G. Snelling, five dollars each, for laudable efforts in saving William P. Fuller and George Holt, who had fallen under the ice in fishing,† $10

* At the meeting in August, of this year, a resolution was adopted, that, "considering the numerous cases, annually presented to the notice of the Society, of men and boys losing their lives from ignorance of the art of swimming, and believing it to be fully within the objects of this Society to aid the means of preventing death, as well as to resuscitate those in whom animation is suspended, the Trustees view with peculiar pleasure the establishment of a Swimming School in this city, under the charge of Dr. Leiber," and with a recommendation to the inhabitants of Boston to avail themselves of the opportunity now afforded to acquire the practical knowledge of so important an art, they appropriated from the funds of the Society one hundred dollars, for the instruction of such a number of pupils as Dr. Leiber might be willing to receive. A committee from the Trustees was accordingly appointed to confer with the Mayor and Aldermen of the city, to invite their concurrence, and also with Dr. Leiber, who expressed his deep sense of the approbation bestowed upon his undertaking by the "Humane Society." And being desirous to receive as many scholars under their grant as he could, without injury to his private pupils, he fixed the number at thirty-six, thus allowing four pupils from each of the public schools in Boston. This proposal was made public through the newspapers, but failed of receiving the attention to which it appears entitled, as only eight scholars availed themselves of the offer.

At the meeting of October, in the same year, the Recording Secretary, agreeably to a former vote, presented an engraved form of "Vote of Thanks," with suitable devices, to be signed by the President and Secretary, and to be presented in the name of the Society, in cases which neither sought nor justified pecuniary compensation, or else as accompaniments to such compensation. Accordingly, in the list of premiums that follow, many instances will be found of such acknowledgments.

† Mr. Inches, to whom the case was committed, having at the same meeting reported a state of facts in reference to the application of one Parker for saving out of

1829. On representation of N. G. Snelling, Esq., there was granted to RICHARD HOSEA, the Society's GOLD MEDAL or a SILVER CUP, for plunging into the water with his clothes on, and rescuing a son of Mr. Joseph Bassett, who had fallen from Tilley's Wharf, $10

To WILLIAM ALLEN, for generous exertions in saving a person who had fallen into the water from Russia Wharf, (though declining to make application for a premium,) a SILVER MEDAL, or the Society's certificate of thanks.

To SILAS SEAVER, and two others, who, as stated by Capt. William Porter, had, at the peril of their own lives, saved John Green, accidentally fallen from the steamboat Connecticut, near Nahant, five dollars each, $15

To STEPHEN TWIST, for rescuing three men who were upset in a boat near Fort Pickering, Salem, on the 9th of July last; and who also had incurred some hazard in endeavoring to save a little boy at another time, $15

To JAMES HYDE, Jr., for heroic exertions, as attested by Mr. George Fuller, in saving his son, a lad of ten years old, at imminent hazard, a GOLD MEDAL, of the value of $10

To PETER BROWN, for saving, with much meritorious effort, the life of Eliza Hedgeman, $5

To ALPHEUS SPEAR, of Quincy, for his exertions in rescuing E. Bell, John Delano, Jr., and a little boy, 9 years of age, when in danger of drowning, by the upsetting of a boat near Quincy, a GOLD MEDAL, or, at his option, $10

the water one Joseph Foster, and it appearing doubtful whether the said Foster *had ever fallen in*, it was voted, *nemine contradicente*, that no premium be awarded.

Also, *a declaration under oath* having been made before a Justice of the Peace, at Lechmere Point, purporting that Joseph Gilson, with three others, had taken James Hedly from Miller's River, but it appearing that no peril was incurred, and no exertions made but such as common humanity would demand, no compensation was allowed.

To ANDREW EATON, for perilous exertions in saving the life of a son of Capt. Nathan Blood, who had fallen from Crowninshield's Wharf, in Salem, Nov. 10th, a MEDAL, or $10

To BENJAMIN OLIVER, ELISHA B. WITHERALL, and ELISHA H. BAKER, a SILVER MEDAL each, and the Society's certificate, for saving the lives of Joseph Smith and three others, seamen, the only survivors of eight, who were upset at sea in Lat. 42 50, Lon. 63, on the 4th of September last.

These survivors were landed at Wellfleet, from the schooner Maria, Capt. Henry Baker, to whom the Trustees voted the Society's certificate of thanks, for his kindness and attention to the sufferers.

N. B. At the same meeting of the Trustees, Dec. 1829, six other premiums of less amount were awarded, on the report of the respective committees.

1830. To JOHN BRUCE, for saving, at great hazard, the officers and crew of the Peruvian, when driven on the rocks on the night of the 17th of March, a piece of plate, with suitable inscriptions, to the value of $20

Also to SUMNER LAWRENCE, who assisted Mr. Bruce, a piece of plate, $15

To SAMUEL CRAIG, for exertions in rescuing three female children, in danger of drowning, $10

1831. To WILLIAM MORTON, a seaman, who, at the most imminent peril, in a heavy gale, boarded the wreck of the schooner Hallet, Dec. 11th, and rescued Heman McLeod, a seaman, the only person left on board, $20

To Mrs. HOPKINS, a passenger on board the packet from Ellsworth, for meritorious exertions, when the vessel was wrecked off Cohasset a few days previous, $10

To JOHN BARKER, HENRY J. TURNER, ESQ., JOHN J. LOTHROP

NATHANIEL HOOPER, Jr., and four others, recommended by Rev. Jacob Flint, for humane and effectual efforts in rescuing the perishing crew of the schooner Boston, wrecked upon Cohasset Rocks, a GOLD MEDAL of the value of ten dollars each, $80

To MR. WEATHERBEE, for rescuing from imminent peril a young boy, $10

1832. To WILLIAM JOHNSON, for saving two men by the name of Phillips, at the imminent hazard of his own life, $20

To MR. JAMES BEERS, of Chatham, in acknowledgment of his singular skill, courage, and benevolence, by which, with the blessing of Divine Providence, *fifteen* persons were rescued from imminent danger, in a night of extreme severity, and when their condition seemed hopeless — the certificate of the thanks of the Trustees, and a donation of $50

To CAPT. COLLINS and his two men, for humane exertions in saving Mr. Seth Thaxter and two others, $20

To JAMES LEONARD, for having at much hazard rescued Mr. William Welsh, $10

Other applications were made at the same time, which, having been duly considered, were dismissed, as not entitled to the notice of the Trustees.

To ISAAC SPRAGUE, for much personal labor and humane exertion in rescuing a man, who had fallen from his boat, $10

1833. It appearing, on representation of William Goddard, Esq., that JAMES SMALLEY, WILLIAM BUSH, JOSIAH COOK, with *nine* others, inhabitants of Provincetown, did, on the first day of December last, by humane and intrepid exertions, take from the wreck of the ship Warren, when cast ashore on Cape Cod, the two mates, six seamen, and a boy, the only survivors of the crew, together with the lifeless body of the captain, and of one of his men, who had perished in the rigging: And it also appearing, that these benevolent individuals received the persons saved into their families, and having treated them with great kindness for several days, furnished them gratuitously with a passage to Boston, when sufficiently recovered to depart:—Therefore it was voted, unanimously, to present twelve dollars, either in money or in a gold medal, to each of the individuals who saved the crew; and three dollars, in addition, to each of those who with exemplary kindness received them into their houses, $162

To JOSEPH TOLMAN, for saving the life of a boy, fallen into the water, $10

1834. A communication was this day, Jan. 3d, presented. stating the humane and generous efforts of JOHN GROZIER and T. SMALL, assisted by Mr. PAINE, in rescuing a crew of a vessel in imminent danger. And it appearing that Mr. Paine, by the upsetting of the boat, in which he had embarked, lost his life, leaving behind a widow and children destitute—therefore it was voted that fifty dollars be presented to the widow, and that ten dollars, or the Society's GOLD MEDAL, be given to each of the individuals instrumental in saving the crew, $70

To GEORGE P. TEWKSBURY, Captain of the Quarantine Boat, for saving the life of a child in imminent danger, $10

To GEORGE W. ADAMS, for saving three men, the value of a GOLD MEDAL, with three dollars for the loss of a part of his clothes, $13

1835. To JOHN L. BRITTON, JOHN PEASLEY, and two others, for humane and perilous exertions in saving Hervey M. Briggs from drowning in the harbor, the sum of forty dollars, divided according to their respective merits; the largest share of which to be given to Britton, $40

To SUSAN FISHER, of Medford, for rescuing her brother and sister from peril, $10

To ADOLPHE BENJAMIN HERMIEUX, a French lad, (on representation of John W. Langdon, Esq.,) who jumped from his vessel into the water, with his clothes on, and saved an American Boy, a GOLD MEDAL, and the Society's certificate of approbation for his generous conduct.*

1836. On the representation of Captain Phelps, of the brig Regulator, that he and his crew were saved from death by the kind and intrepid exertions of the officers and crew of the brig Cervantes, when shipwrecked, on the 5th of February last — it was voted, unanimously, that a GOLD MEDAL, with ten dollars in money, be presented to the captain and each of the crew, nine in number, of the Cervantes; and that the letter of Capt. Phelps be published, with the view of procuring aid for the survivors of the shipwreck. The whole sum voted was $180

To two boys, of the name of CARTWRIGHT and WHITE, for saving a third, when under the ice, a GOLD MEDAL each. $20

On recommendation of Capt. Rider, a GOLD MEDAL was given to the mate of his vessel, and $7 each to two of his men, for their exertions in saving seven men from the schooner Aurora, wrecked off Cape Hatteras, Feb. 2, $24

To SHUBAEL COTTLE, for his generous efforts to save the life of Capt. Uriel Mayhew, of the schooner George, a GOLD MEDAL, of the value of $20

To JAMES and JOSHUA Y. BEERS, on representation of Andrew L. Simpson, for saving the lives of all on board of the ship Mercury, when wrecked off Nantucket, a medal each, $20

1837. Two Greeks belonging to the brig Alexandros, having saved the life of a child, on the 7th of September, and the

* We have heard, through a gentleman acquainted with the friends of young Hermieux, of the very high estimation in which this medal, and the accompanying document, are held by his family in France.

President, upon learning that they were about departing from the country, having presented, to each of them, a GOLD MEDAL, in the name of the Society, it was voted, unanimously, to confirm the grant, $20

To JOSEPH STEVENS, a lad of 16 years of age, in the employ of Jones, Lows, & Ball, for saving a boy from drowning, a SILVER MEDAL, $5

To JOHN L. BRITTON, for rescuing, at the hazard of his own life, a little girl, who had fallen into the water from the Mill Dam, a GOLD MEDAL, $10

To JAMES DOLLIVER, for saving from drowning a young boy, named Stearns, $7

To JAMES P. HARVEY, for rescuing a child, at much personal hazard, a GOLD MEDAL, $10

To EMANUEL JACKSON, for saving a lad of seven years old, fallen from Sargent's Wharf, $7

To Mrs. ELIZABETH BRYAN, for rescuing, at some personal peril, a little child from a clay-pit, $4

To JOSEPH LUCAS, of Plymouth, for saving a boy in danger of drowning, $10

To HENRY DEARBORN, for saving the life of a lad, in danger of perishing in the Frog Pond, a GOLD MEDAL of the value of $10

Also, to the very destitute mother of said lad, $3

1838. To RUFUS BECKFORD, on representation of Mr. G. Stanley, for saving a boy, who had fallen from the Eastern packet, $10

To WILLIAM MILLS, for saving, at some risk, a boy from drowning in a pond at South Boston, $5

To WARREN REED, and SAMUEL BROWN, two lads, of Salem, for rescuing, with much heroic exertion, a young son of Mr. John Marks, the Society's GOLD MEDAL, each $20

To JAMES SAURIN, for rescuing young Martin Bates from drowning, July 27th, $5

To ABRAHAM RICH, for saving, by great exertions, a man and three women, who were clinging to a boat, upset near Deer Island, a GOLD MEDAL of the value of $20

1839. To JOHN KENT, for saving one of the crew of the Revenue Cutter, $7

To MICHAEL WILSON, for a similar effort of humanity, $8

To LANGFORD W. LORING, for saving two boys, who had fallen through the ice, $5

To EDWARD ARMSTRONG, WM. S. HUTCHINS, JOHN GROZER, and DANIEL SMITH, for rescuing, at the peril of their own lives, the officers and crew of the brig Lucy Ann, of Portland, wrecked near Truro, a GOLD MEDAL of ten dollars, to each, together with the Society's certificate, in approbation of their generous efforts, $40

To ROBERT CORRAN, on recommendation of M. Brimmer, Esq., for intrepid exertions in saving a boy, who had fallen from Commercial Wharf, $15

To J. L. PROUTY, of the Revenue Cutter, and to J. CURTIS, assisting him, for their successful efforts, as represented by Capt. J. Sturgis, in rescuing Laurence Hickey, when fallen under the ice — a GOLD MEDAL each, $20

To GEORGE F. COVERLY, for saving, at much hazard, a lad from drowning, $15

To SAMUEL K. BAILEY, on representation of William Hayden, Jr., for rescuing, at imminent peril, Mr. Murphy, fallen overboard, the Society's GOLD MEDAL, $15

[Mr. Murphy soon afterwards died in consequence of the exposure.]

To a lad named W. F. MILLER, for saving a child, who had fallen from Doak's Wharf, $10

To PATRICK and LEVI GILMAN, for saving two men from drowning, and recovering the dead body of another, five dollars each, $10

To JONATHAN COLLINS, of Truro, for having risked his life, to save five persons, belonging to Provincetown, and who, having been upset in a boat, must have perished, but for his assistance. $10

To CUSHING HORTON, and three others, crew of the fishing schooner Xyphian, for saving five persons clinging to a wreck, five dollars each, $20

To WILLIAM P. BOWEN, ship carpenter, for jumping from a wharf, and rescuing a child, $10

To CAPT. BENJAMIN ANDREWS, keeper of the Light House near Sandy Bay, for having, at imminent peril, saved two men who were clinging to the masts of a boat, which had upset and was sinking under them, the Society's GOLD MEDAL, and to his WIFE and DAUGHTER, assisting him, three dollars each, $16

1840. To JOSEPH HOWARD, SAMUEL PARKER, and seven others, for boarding the wreck of the brig Independence, during the heavy gale of 15th Dec. last, and taking thence the crew from the rigging, at much hazard, five dollars each, $45

To ISAAC SMALL, who, during the same severe gale, went on board the brig Austin, wrecked at Provincetown, and at the peril of his own life, and by signal exertions, rescued a disabled seaman, the President was authorized to present a QUADRANT, with a suitable inscription, in token of approbation of his heroic conduct.

To GORHAM RIGGS, DOAND RYDER, and nine other persons, who, during the same dreadful tempest of Dec. 15th, went on board a vessel in Gloucester Harbor, and were the means, under Divine Providence, of saving several persons, five dollars each, $55

To S. Norbery, captain of a Swedish vessel, and also to his Mate, for their humane exertions in saving the crew of a disabled vessel, at sea, a Gold Medal each, $20

To Samuel Pierce, and his Son, for assistance rendered to the crew of the schooner Scio, when driven on shore at Wellfleet, in the gale of 15th December, five dollars, $10

To Benjamin Heath, on representation of Rev. Sebastian Streeter, for heroic and successful exertions in saving a woman, who had thrown herself into the water near Warren Bridge, $20

To Charles E. Pitman, for saving from drowning a child of Mr. Brown, who had fallen into deep water, near the Lowell Railroad, and must have perished but for the heroic exertions of Mr. Pitman, a Gold Medal, $20

To Peter Murphy, of Charlestown, on representation of C. Tyler, Steward of the McLean Asylum, for rescuing Mary Ann Crarie, who had fallen from the Charlestown Branch Railroad, and must otherwise have perished, $10

To Sewall Reed, for saving from drowning a boy sixteen years of age, near Battery Wharf, $10

To James W. Newcomb, for exertions in a similar case, as represented by Mr. Samuel Prince, $8

To Aaron L. Sargent and Kilby P. Sargent, who, on representation of the Selectmen of Gloucester, had ventured through the breakers, in a boat, and at some hazard had saved Capt. George Murdock from his schooner, stranded on the Bar, five dollars each, $10

To George Brown, for saving from drowning, Mary Ormond, of Charlestown, $5

1841. To George S. Fogg, on representation of Amos Tufts, for rescuing from drowning a deranged person, who, on leaving the Lowell Cars, had jumped into Charles River, $10

To CHARLES R. CHENEY, of Lowell, on statement of Rev. U. C. Burnap, for rescuing two boys from drowning, $10

To ADIN ALLEN, of Springfield, on representation of Rev. B. C. Cutler, for his heroic exertions in saving a person from drowning, in Connecticut River, the Society's GOLD MEDAL, and their certificate of thanks, $10

To JAMES PAXTER, for rescuing a child, at much personal risk, who had fallen overboard near Lewis Wharf, a GOLD MEDAL, $10

To JOHN BROWN, a fisherman, who, according to certificate of Hon. Judge Prescott, and others, had during a severe squall ventured out in a small boat, a mile and an half from Nahant, and rescued three persons in great peril, from the upsetting of their boat, the Society's GOLD MEDAL, $10

To MIDSHIPMAN CHARLES WESTON, for his gallant conduct in jumping overboard to the rescue of a man, who had thrown himself from the ship Columbus, in a fit of delirium tremens, a GOLD MEDAL, $10

To CHARLES F. SMITH, for saving the life of Charles F. Bradford, $5

To JOHN POOL, for rescuing a little girl from drowning, near the Marine Railway, $4

To J. WHEELER, for saving, at the imminent peril of his own life, George Hatch, a boy who had fallen overboard, a GOLD MEDAL of the value of $10

To ARCHIBALD SMITH, who saved a little child, of three years old, $5

And to PATRICK CAVANAGH, for saving another, $5

1842. To MILTON HALL, Jr., for having, with great exertions and much hazard, saved a man who had fallen into Charles River, the Society's GOLD MEDAL, and ten dollars in money, $20

[Mr. Hall had previously been the instrument of saving the lives of two lads, when in great peril.]

To Mr. JOHN PORTER, for saving a child from drowning, in the Dock, near Commercial Wharf, $10

To BAYAN CORLAND, for humane efforts in saving Gerry Stafflin, as attested by John P. Langdon, $10

Also, to his SON, for aiding him, $5

To GEORGE FOGG, who jumped overboard and rescued from drowning a lad named Burrill, the same individual having twice before been the means of saving life, (see 1841,) $10

To ALEXANDER REDMAN, who had jumped overboard and saved from drowning a son of Mr. Jones, Atkinson street, $10

To EDWARD POWERS, for a similar act of humanity, and with greater personal hazard, a GOLD MEDAL, $10

To C. F. STEBBINS, for rescuing a boy from drowning in the Dock, at Sargent's Wharf, $7

To WILLIAM W. PERKINS, who, with heroic courage, jumped from the end of Comey's Wharf, an height of 15 feet, and rescued from drowning a lad, who had already been long in the water, and was senseless, a GOLD MEDAL, $10

To MR. T. S. GREENWOOD, keeper of the Light House at Ipswich, and to JOSEPH MARSHALL, for noble exertions in saving the survivors from the wreck of the schooner Deposit, driven on Lakeman's Ledge in a severe gale, Dec. 23, 1839, a GOLD MEDAL each, $20

[The survivors thus rescued, were Mrs. Cotterill, the wife of the captain, George Emery, and Chandler Mahoney. Captain Cotterill, with three others, perished.]

To MARTIN WINCH, a lad of 16 years, who saved the life of a child three years of age, who had fallen from a wharf at South Boston, a GOLD MEDAL, of the value of $10

1843. To W. R. Tuck, Benja. F. Merrill, and Thomas Little, for saving, at much hazard, three seamen of the British steamer Caledonia, when upset in a boat at midnight during a violent storm, five dollars each, $15

To Capt. Ezekiel Darling, of Marblehead, a Gold Medal, and to John Gardner, and four others, seamen, five dollars each, for their exertions in rescuing the crew and passengers of the brig John Hancock, of Quincy, wrecked on Tinker's Island, near Marblehead, March 17th, $35

To Ezra Brown, and Nathan Boynton, who, at the hazard of their lives, saved from drowning a woman, who attempted suicide by jumping from a wharf near Charlestown Bridge, ten dollars to the former, and to the latter, seven, $17

To Benjamin Buckley, who saved the life of a boy, who fell into the water, July 16th, near South Boston Bridge, $8

To Isaiah Harding, the captain, six dollars, and to each of the six men composing the crew of the Life-Boat at Chatham, for their services in attempting to rescue, at much hazard, the crew of the brig President, in May last, four dollars each, $30

1844. To John C. Nichols, for his successful exertions in saving, at the risk of his own life, a little girl who had fallen from the Eastern Steamboat Wharf, a Gold Medal, $10

To John Carlin, for generous efforts in saving the life of a little boy, James Denny, who had broken through the ice, near Liverpool Wharf, a Gold Medal, $10

To Thomas S. Harman, for saving from drowning a child named Charles Nichols, fallen from a wharf, a Gold Medal, $10

To Patrick Welch, for saving, at some risk, the life of William Redmond, $7

To Samuel Hill, for rescuing from drowning a lad, fallen overboard near the Eastern Railroad Depot, a Medal, of the value of $10

To Capt. Cobb, for jumping from the deck of his vessel, and saving a lad from drowning, the Society's Medal, $10

To Moses B. Tower, John W. Tower, William James, and five others, for their humane and heroic exertions in saving, by the Life-Boat of the Society, stationed at Hull, the officers and crew of the brig Tremont, of New York, wrecked on Point Alderton Bar in a violent gale, on Monday, Oct. 7, ten dollars in money to each, together with the Society's Gold Medal to Capt. Tower, in token of the approbation of the Trustees of his and their meritorious conduct, $90

1845. To nine of the first crew of the Society's boat at Hull, for their gallant though unsuccessful attempt to rescue those on board the ship Massasoit, wrecked on 11th of December, at Point Alderton, $90

To seven of the crew of the Society's boat at Hull, who made a second gallant and successful attempt and succeeded in rescuing Captain Berry and eleven others, from the ship Massasoit, wrecked at Point Alderton, Dec. 11th, $105

To Greely Stevenson Curtis, for his gallant and successful exertions in rescuing a youth from drowning among the ice in the Back Bay, in Boston, a Gold Medal, and a certificate of the Society.

1846. To the captains and crews of the Humane Society's boats at Nantucket, for their gallant and successful exertions in rescuing the officers and crew of the brig Mariner, wrecked off Nantucket: To Captain Heman Eldridge, a Gold Medal. To his crew, George Fisher, Joseph Perry, Hiram Fisher, Jesse Eldridge, and William Patterson, a Silver Medal, each.

To Capt. Eben Gould, a Gold Medal. To his crew, Moses Hamilton, Theophilus Key, John Hale, Henry Young, and Meltiah Fisher, a Silver Medal, each.

To CHARLES O. H. HILL, for signal exertions in rescuing William Sheir from drowning, $10

To WILLIAM SHEIR, for signal exertions in endeavoring to save William Thompson from drowning. $10

To P. BAYLE, for signal exertions in rescuing John Carney from drowning, $5

1847. To MR. CUMMINGS, for his gallant and successful exertions in saving human life, a GOLD MEDAL.

To SILAS HALE, of Stowe, for signal exertions in saving T. Bucker from drowning, $10

To F. E. JACKSON, for signal exertions in saving William Bennett from drowning, $5

1848. To IVORY B. GOODWIN, for signal exertions in rescuing William O. Brian from drowning, $5

To ROBERT MILLIKEN, for signal exertions in rescuing M. C. Driscoll from drowning, $10

To DR. PARKMAN, for signal exertions in rescuing John Collins from drowning, $5

1849. To ROBERT B. FORBES, since Vice-President of the Humane Society, for gallant and successful efforts in saving life at the wreck of the ship Charles Bartlett, in the Atlantic ocean, a GOLD MEDAL.

To the Society's crew, W. R. BLOWER, T. ELLIS, A. NYE, B. ATWOOD, D. NYE, and S. HARDING, for their signal and successful efforts in rescuing the crew of the schooner Only Daughter, of Lubeck, Maine, $35

To CAPT. JAMES CUNNINGHAM, of the ship Riga, for his signal and humane exertions in saving life, a SILVER MEDAL.

To JOSEPH HARDING, for signal exertions in saving life in the case of the Franklin, $10

To six men of the Franklin, for their gallant and successful efforts in saving life, a SILVER MEDAL each.

To MULFORD RICH, for signal exertions in saving human life, $20

NOTE. — From the time of the foundation of the Society, 1786, to the year 1849, it will be seen by this record, that the Humane Society had conferred ONE HUNDRED AND SIXTEEN GOLD MEDALS. Since 1849, it has been the custom of the Society to present their new Silver Medal, as the highest award it is in their power to give, and equivalent to the presentation of the Gold Medal of former times, which was conferred when the rescuer showed uncommon courage and perseverance in saving human life at the risk of his own.

1850. To five men of the Society's Life-Boat at Plymouth, for signal exertions in saving life from a wreck, $25

To WILLIAM W. HOOPER, for signal exertions in saving human life, $5

To T. MAHONEY, for signal exertions in saving human life, $20

To I. HAYDEN, and D. STODDARD, for signal exertions in rescuing the crew of the shipwrecked brig L'Essai, $10

To six men of the Society's Life-Boat at Cohasset, for signal exertions in saving the crew of the St. John, wrecked on Minot's Ledge, $30

1851. To THOMAS JEFFERSON ALLEN, for gallant and successful efforts in rescuing Francis Devereux from drowning, a SILVER MEDAL.

To THOMAS VALLEY, of East Boston, for gallant and successful efforts in saving human life, a SILVER MEDAL.

To BENJ. TUFTS, for signal exertions in saving a youth from drowning at India Wharf, $10

1852. To W. CHAMPLIN, I. CURTIS, W. T. MURPHY, and W. SIBLEY, of the Pilot Boat Yankee, for their gallant and successful efforts in rescuing lives from a wreck, a SILVER MEDAL each.

To MR. LORD and MR. HAMILTON, for their signal and humane exertions in aid of the bark Josepha, $10

To I. L. KEHEW, of Salem, for his gallant and successful exertions in saving human life, a SILVER MEDAL.

1853. To W. MCARDLE, for signal exertions in saving human life, $3

To THOMAS COURTNEY, for signal and humane exertions in saving human life, a BRONZE MEDAL.

To E. STOREY, for signal exertions in saving human life, $5

1854. To I. L. HATCH, for signal and humane exertions in rescuing Herbert Murphy from drowning, $20

To E. HOLMES, captain, and four of the crew of the Society's Life-Boat at Duxbury, for signal exertions in rescuing the shipwrecked brig Valasco, $30

To six men of the crew of the Society's Life Boat of Chatham, for signal and humans exertions in saving human life, $30

To JAMES GIBB, I. M. MCLEAN, and W. R. THYNE, of the Three Bells, for their gallant and successful efforts in saving human life, a SILVER MEDAL each.

To EDWARD MELLEN, and I. W. MARSHALL, of the ship San Francisco, for gallant and successful efforts in saving human life, a SILVER MEDAL each.

To E. T. LOWE, JAMES CREIGHTON, JAMES T. WATKINS, G. C. STANFORD, and JOHN F. CROSDELL, of the bark Kelly, for gallant and successful efforts in saving human life, a SILVER MEDAL each.

To JAMES SAVAGE, for gallant and successful efforts in saving human life in the case of the brig Elizabeth, a SILVER MEDAL.

To CHARLES B. LUCAS, for gallant and successful efforts in saving human life, a SILVER MEDAL.

To B. W. HOLLIS, for gallant and successful efforts in saving human life, a SILVER MEDAL.

1855. To MICHAEL BARRETT, for gallant and successful efforts in saving a child from drowning, a SILVER MEDAL.

To GEORGE M. OLMSTEAD, for gallant and successful efforts in saving human life, a SILVER MEDAL.

To CHARLES WAGNER, for signal exertions in saving human life, $15

1856. To nine men of the schooner Favorite, of Marblehead, for signal and humane exertions in saving human life, a BRONZE MEDAL each.

To T. MCCARTY, for signal exertions in saving human life, $5

To W. A. COOPER, of Scituate, for signal exertions in saving human life. $5

To GEORGE TEWKSBURY, and CHARLES S. TEWKSBURY, for signal exertions in saving human life. $10

[The family of Tewksbury, of Deer Island, have up to this time saved the lives of thirty-three persons, and their humane exertions have been repeatedly acknowledged by the Humane Society.]

1857. To twenty-four men who, on January 20th, assisted in rescuing the crew of the ship Californian, wrecked near Cohasset, $48

To MRS. MARY ANNE KIMBALL, of Cohasset, for her generous and humane conduct towards the shipwrecked crew of the ship Californian, a CERTIFICATE.

To the crew of the Humane Society's Life-Boat at Annisquam, for the rescue of the schooner Scion, $40

To JONATHAN SNOW, for his gallant and successful efforts in rescuing the crew of the Ellen Maria, a SILVER MEDAL.

To D. S. LINNELL, for his gallant and successful efforts in rescuing the crew of the ship Orissa, a SILVER MEDAL.

To the Humane Society's boat's crew, for rescue of crews of the Orissa and Ellen Maria, at East Orleans, $60

1858. To GEORGE SNELL, ESQ., for his gallant and successful efforts in the rescue of a man from drowning among the ice at Jamaica Pond, a SILVER MEDAL.

To EDWARD WARD, and JOHN L. SAVAGE, for their humane and successful efforts in rescuing two young men from drowning among the ice on the Back Bay, $16

To L. S. FICKETT, of Millbridge, for his humane and successful efforts in rescuing Catharine McLaughlin from drowning, $5

1859. To EDWARD LARY, and FRANCIS MCGUIRE, for humane and successful efforts in rescuing from drowning two boys, to each a BRONZE MEDAL.

To MISS ELIZABETH WHITMORE, for her courageous and successful rescue from drowning, in the Back Bay, of a lad named Brigham, a SILVER MEDAL.

To JOHN S. PARKER, for gallant and successful efforts in rescuing two boys from drowning, a SILVER MEDAL.

To J. M. DOLLIVER and P. H. CHANDLER, for gallant and successful efforts in rescuing from drowning Captain Apter of the schooner Caroline, a SILVER MEDAL each.

To the crew of the Humane Society's Life Boat No. 3, CAPT. THOMAS HUDSON, H. HUDSON, S. GRACE, M. GRACE, C. LINCOLN, E. RICHARDSON, I. HAYDEN, crew, for their humane conduct in rescuing nine men from the British brig Herald, wrecked at Nantasket Beach: to Capt. Hudson a certificate, to the crew $48

To Q. R. MCFIELD, for his gallant and successful efforts in rescuing from drowning George Clarke, a SILVER MEDAL.

1860. To WILLIAM A. ROFF, for his gallant and successful efforts in rescuing from drowning Edgar F. Matthews, a SILVER MEDAL.

To DOMINICUS POOL, Captain, and to the crew of the Humane

Society's Life Boat at Squam Bar, for humane conduct in rescuing the crew of the schooner Magellan Cloud, $25

To JOSEPH PEABODY GARDNER, afterwards the Treasurer of the Humane Society, for his gallant and successful rescue from drowning in the Back Bay of a youth named Clarke, a SILVER MEDAL.

To CAPTAIN JOHN WILSON, of the brig Minnie Sheffer, for his gallant and humane conduct in rescuing six hundred and six persons from the Royal Mail Steamer Connaught, burned at sea, a SILVER MEDAL and the Certificate of the Society.

To the CAPTAIN and crew of the Humane Society's Life Boat at Nantasket, for humane efforts in rescuing eight persons from the wreck of the schooner Nevis, $65

To PHILIP H. FOLGER, for repeated exhibitions of courage and humane conduct on the coast of Nantucket, the Certificate of the Society.

To JOHN FITZGERALD, for his gallant and successful efforts in rescuing Ella Brown from drowning at Boston, a SILVER MEDAL.

1861. To JACOB HITTINGER, for his gallant and successful efforts in rescuing from drowning Herbert E. Johnson, a SILVER MEDAL.

To THREE MEN of the Pilot Boat Friend, for rescuing from drowning Captain James M. Dolliver, $25

To TIMOTHY McINTIRE, a deaf cripple, for his courageous and successful efforts in rescuing from drowning a son of E. G. Martin at Boston, a BRONZE MEDAL.

To CAPTAIN SAMUEL JAMES, of Hull, for his humane and successful efforts in rescuing twelve persons from the ship Maritana, wrecked near Boston Light, the Certificate of the Society.

To H. S. Lich, S. James, G. Kittle, R. S. Hunt, and F. B. Wellock, for their humane and successful efforts in assisting at the rescue of twelve persons from the wreck of the ship Maritana, $50

1862. To John Regan and David McCarty, for their humane efforts in rescuing Cornelius Coonley from drowning, $6

To Michael Casniff, for his humane efforts in rescuing a child from drowning, $2

To Andrew Lally, for his humane efforts in rescuing John Bartlett from drowning, $3

To Robert Torrence, for his humane exertions in rescuing a child from drowning, $3

1863. To Mrs. Lucinda B. Cutter, daughter of General John S. Tyler, for her courage and great presence of mind as displayed in rescuing two young men from drowning at Nahant, a Silver Medal,

To Mr. Luscomb, for his gallant and successful efforts in rescuing a person from drowning, a Silver Medal.

To John Thomas, of Beverly, seaman of U. S. Steamer Katahdin, for his gallant and successful efforts in saving two persons from drowning in the Mississippi River, the Certificate of the Society.

1864. To John Courtney, of East Abington, for his humane and successful efforts in rescuing from drowning a daughter of Henry B. Rogers, Esq., a Certificate and $20

To Col. Samuel M. Quincy, for his gallant and successful efforts in rescuing from drowning in Quincy Bay, Mr. Henderson Inches Dehon, Miss Caroline Dehon, and Mr. Ashburton Webster, a Silver Medal.

To the crew of the Humane Society's Life Boat at Monomoy, for their humane and successful rescue of the crew of the wrecked bark Lagrange, $52

To ROBERT SHAW, for his humane exertions in rescuing from drowning Mr. John Tyler and his son, $6

To CHARLES L. WILLIAMS, FRANCIS WILLIAMS, T. P. STONE, and WILLIAM STONE, who put off in dories in a gale of wind, and rescued five persons, survivors of nine, capsized in Salem Harbor, $10, and a CERTIFICATE to each.

1865. To CORNELIUS O'BRIEN, of Boston, for his humane efforts in rescuing from smothering in a vault, Richard O. Neil, $15

To RALPH BLACK, for his gallant and successful efforts in rescuing from drowning Mary Coleman, at Quincy, and for recovering the body of Catharine Conner, a SILVER MEDAL.

To PHILIP THRASHER, of Marblehead, nine years of age, for his humane and successful efforts in rescuing a child named Holt, six years of age, from drowning, a BRONZE MEDAL.

To FREDERICK REMSDAL, of Nantucket, for his gallant and successful rescue of one of the wrecked crew of the schooner Emeline Treat, a SILVER MEDAL.

To ALFRED MAYO, for gallant and successful efforts in rescuing one of the crew of the Clemantha Hopkins, wrecked on Cape Cod beach, a SILVER MEDAL.

To MICHAEL CORCORAN, of Charlestown, for his humane and successful efforts in rescuing from drowning Michael Townley, $10

1866. To CAPT. ARTHUR F. CLARKE, for his gallant and successful efforts in rescuing from drowning, at Nahant, E. Lindsey Amory, of Boston, a SILVER MEDAL.

To CAPT. EDMUND BURKE, of the brig Fredonia, for his gallant and humane conduct in rescuing the passengers and crew, three hundred and eight in number, of the ship Gratitude, lost at sea.

To Paul Francis Knowles, for his gallant and successful efforts in the rescue of Malvonia Henly from drowning in Boston harbor, a Silver Medal.

To W. C. Lee, of Newton, for his gallant and successful efforts in rescuing Z. T. Cushman, and a youth named Levitt, from drowning in Baptist Pond, a Silver Medal.

To Daniel O'Connell, for his humane and successful efforts in rescuing Elizabeth Duffy from drowning at Boston, $10

To William Falkner, of Boston, for his gallant and successful efforts in rescuing a daughter of Arthur Lithgow Devens from drowning at Nahant, a Silver Medal.

To Samuel T. Hanscomb, of Boston, for his gallant and successful efforts in rescuing the young men Donnelly and Jones from drowning at Cambridge, a Silver Medal.

1867. To H. B. Jones, Captain of the Humane Society's Life Boat at Monument, and his crew, J. B. Lynch, L. B. Briggs, Robert Reany, C. W. Holmes, I. B. Bartlett, P. Bartlett, and C. Reany, for their humane and successful efforts in rescuing the officers and crew of the shipwrecked bark Velma, $100

To Byron Rich and N. B. Holmes, for their gallant and successful efforts in rescuing two children of Mrs. E. A. F. Cook from drowning at Quincy, a Silver Medal each.

To Dudley D. Davis, of Salem, for his gallant and successful efforts in rescuing from drowning Edward and Henry Tucker, a Silver Medal. [Within twenty years Mr. Davis has rescued from drowning sixteen men and one woman.]

To Capt. John Giles, of Humane Society's Life Boat at Rockport, and his crew, W. Grimes, A. Grimes, S. York, G. Cleary, I. Hurley, and I. Hobbs, for their humane and successful efforts in rescuing the officers and crew of the wrecked schooner Addie Low, $70

1868. To BRIDGET MARY O'TOOLE, for her courageous and successful efforts in rescuing Jane Devlin from drowning at Nahant, a SILVER MEDAL.

To WILLIAM H. BURROUGHS, for his gallant and successful efforts in rescuing E. H. Pierce and P. Scanland from drowning at Charlestown, a SILVER MEDAL.

To JOHN FINNIGAN, a lad of twelve years of age, for his humane and successful efforts in rescuing two boys from drowning at Boston, $5

To JOHN J. LANNIN, for his humane and successful efforts in rescuing Hugh Shield from drowning at Rowe's Wharf, $5

1869. To DANIEL DONALY, for his humane and successful efforts in rescuing Edward Hatch from drowning at Boston, a BRONZE MEDAL.

To AMBROSE WHITE, DANIEL PARSONS, ISAAC MORSE, and JOSEPH HILLUR, for their gallant and successful efforts in going in a gale of wind, and at great peril, to the rescue of the crew of the yacht Edith, wrecked near Gloucester, a SILVER MEDAL each.

To JAMES ROWE, for his humane and successful efforts in rescuing G. M. Paul, I. E. Giles, and G. S. Giles, from drowning at Rockport. Mr. Rowe elected to take a Certificate.

1870. To STEPHEN O. SCHOFF, for his gallant and successful efforts in rescuing two sons of W. H. C. Hayden, of Newtonville, from drowning, a SILVER MEDAL.

To LIEUT. ZALINSKI, United States Army, for his gallant and successful efforts in rescuing a soldier from drowning in Boston Harbor, the Certificate of the Society.

To PRIVATE MICHAEL BROWN, United States Army, for his gallant and successful efforts in rescuing a fellow soldier from drowning in Boston Harbor, a BRONZE MEDAL.

To JAMES CUTHBURTSON, for his gallant and successful efforts in rescuing Franklin Snow, Jr., from drowning at Commercial Wharf, Boston, a SILVER MEDAL.

To MRS. HARRIET TRIMBLE, for her courageous and humane efforts in rescuing Thomas McLaughlin from drowning at Hull, $10 and the Certificate of the Society.

To LIEUT. COMMANDER N. M. DYER, United States Navy, of Melrose, for his gallant and successful efforts in plunging into the sea from the United States ship Ossipee, in rough weather, and rescuing one of his crew from drowning, a SILVER MEDAL.

1871. To LIEUT. GEORGE WILSON, for his gallant and successful efforts in rescuing two sons of P. Foster from drowning at Lawrence, a SILVER MEDAL.

To A. FANNING, I. GARDNER, I. HAMBLIN, G. A. VEDDER, H. C. COFFIN, W. M. BATES, J. HOLMES, and S. KEY, for their gallant and successful efforts in the rescue of the crew of the schooner Mary Anne, wrecked among the ice on Nantucket Bar. The steamer Island Home had made an unsuccessful effort to rescue the crew, when it was effected with boats. A SILVER MEDAL and $10 to each.

To T. S. SANBURY, I. FISHER, H. C. COFFIN, J. G. SMITH, I. P. DUNTON, I. G. APPLETON, J. P. COFFIN, and V. SMALL, for their humane and successful efforts in rescuing the crew of the schooner Mary H. Banks, wrecked off Nantucket, $68

To CAPTAIN J. A. JAMES, of Humane Society's Nantasket Beach Life Boat, and his crew, WM. JAMES, FRANCIS JAMES, BENJAMIN POPE, JAMES LOW, JAMES POPE, ALONZO MITCHELL, JOHN AUGUSTUS, and GEORGE AUGUSTUS, for their gallant and successful efforts in rescuing the crew of the schooner W. R. Georn, wrecked on Nantasket Dec. 23, 1870, $95

1872. To JOHN S. TROWBRIDGE, for his gallant and successful efforts in rescuing James Crowley from drowning in Mystic Pond, a SILVER MEDAL.

To CAPTAIN B. S. CROMWELL, for his humane and successful efforts in rescuing the crew of the schooner White Swan, wrecked off Cape Pogue, the Certificate of the Society.

To C. H. LOVETT, for his gallant and successful efforts in rescuing Mrs. Adams from drowning at Cohasset Narrows, a SILVER MEDAL.

To EDWARD COLT, for his humane and successful efforts in rescuing three men from drowning in Massapoag Pond, the Certificate of the Society.

1873. To WILLIAM DINDEN, for the gallant and successful efforts of himself and his crew G. FULLER, H. R. COBB, and M. EVANS, in rescuing the crew of the schooner Anna Maria, capsized off Thacher Island;—to Captain Dinden a SILVER MEDAL; to his crew, $50

To S. A. SMITH, who led the party, and to C. C. CHURCH, ORIN KEENY, and WM. VEDDER, who went on the first attempt, and to IRA LINES, who went on the second attempt, and to WM. HASKINS, H. I. ALLEN, and F. S. ALLEN, who went on the third attempt, for their gallant and successful efforts in rescuing the crew of the schooner Mary Grain, wrecked on Nashawena;—to S. A. Smith a SILVER MEDAL; to the crew, $120

To Dr. JOHN COLLINS WARREN, for his gallant attempt, at the imminent peril of his own life, to save a youth from drowning among the ice at Ward's Pond, a SILVER MEDAL.

To HERBERT T. SHAW, for his gallant and successful efforts in rescuing James Welch from drowning at Ward's Pond, a SILVER MEDAL.

To HARRIET C. DAVIS, for her humane exertions in assisting at the rescue of Quasett, a Certificate.

To D. F. LARKIN, Jr., ALBERT CRANDALL, I. S. CRANDALL, B. GREENE, J. HARVEY, COURTLAND GAVIT, EUGENE NASH, EDWIN NASH, and W. NASH, for their humane efforts at the wreck of the steamer Metis, off Watch Hill, a Certificate each.

To REV. MR. ANCIENT, for his noble and humane efforts at the wreck of the steamer Atalanta, off Halifax, a Certificate.

To MARY ANNE KEYES, for her courageous and judicious conduct at the late fire on Hanover street, whereby a number of women were saved from being burned to death or from serious injury, a SILVER MEDAL.

1874. To HOWARD HOPPIN, of Providence, for signal exertions in rescuing Charles L. Perkins and a lad named Pillsbury, from drowning in Big Turkey Pond, a Certificate.

To PATRICK SULLIVAN, Quartermaster United States frigate Wabash, for signal exertions in rescuing from drowning at sea, seaman Westphail, a Certificate.

To ROBERT RENSSELAER FULLER, and SYLVESTER RUSSELL CROCKER, for signal and humane exertions in rescuing Captain I. F. Adams of Cotuit, a BRONZE MEDAL each.

To MIDSHIPMAN LUCIAN YOUNG, United States Navy, for signal and humane exertions in rescuing from drowning seaman James Anderson, a Certificate.

To JOHN LANGDON, for gallant and successful endeavors in rescuing James O'Brien, a SILVER MEDAL.

To CAPTAIN N. E. GLOVER, for gallant and successful endeavors in rescuing Francis Packard from drowning, a SILVER MEDAL.

1875. To the crew of the Society's Life Boat at Quidit, for humane exertions in the rescue of the crew of the William Henry, $4 each.

To DENNIS MCCARTHY, for gallant and successful efforts in rescuing five persons from drowning near Fort Winthrop, a SILVER MEDAL.

To WALTER S. PEMBER, for gallant and successful endeavors in rescuing Mr. John Taylor from drowning, a SILVER MEDAL.

To FRANCIS E. GREEN, and MISS LINA F. COE, for signal and humane exertions in rescuing Jesse E. Cole from drowning, the Certificate of the Society to each.

To CAPT. CHARLES THOMAS, of the British steamer Greece, for humane conduct in rescuing James Austin and George Roberts, and for bringing to this country 400 persons from the wrecked ship Europa, the Certificate of the Society.

To I. A. WYMAN, for his gallant and successful efforts in rescuing Mrs. G. A. Colburn from drowning in a well at Lowell, a SILVER MEDAL.

To H. C. NYE, Master United States Navy, and to J. L. HENSIKER, Master United States Navy, for gallant and successful efforts in rescuing Lieut. James Franklin from drowning, a SILVER MEDAL each.

1876. To I. MORRIS MEREDITH, RICHARD C. HURD, and EDWARD ROBBINS WHARTON, for gallant and successful efforts in rescuing Mary Elinor Perkins and Charles B. Perkins from drowning in Jamaica Pond, a SILVER MEDAL each.

To JAMES G. ABBOTT, for gallant and successful efforts in rescuing Robert Davis and William Bertram from drowning at Lawrence, a SILVER MEDAL.

To WILLIAM PEPPER, for humane exertions in rescuing several persons blown into the water by the late explosion of gas at South Boston, a BRONZE MEDAL.

To SIMEON T. HALL, for gallant and successful efforts in rescuing W. B. Goff from drowning, a SILVER MEDAL.

To NORMAN B. SCRIBNER, for gallant and successful efforts in rescuing Caroline M. Clark from drowning, a SILVER MEDAL.

To CAPTAIN D. L. GIFFORD, of the ship Young Phœnix, for his generous and humane conduct at the time of his rescue of the passengers and crew of the British ship Strathmore, wrecked on the Crozet Islands, the Certificate of the Society.

APPENDIX.

EARLY MEMBERS.

A salute from the Castle, with "the Governor's barge to accompany them," may seem in these times a somewhat superfluous demonstration of respect to a charitable society, not yet incorporated, on its customary tour of duty. But those were days of ceremony and salutes. French officers were among us, the ancient manners were not forgotten, and Governor Hancock perfectly understood the characters of the men for whom he ordered that token of respect. In truth, among the founders and early promoters of this Society were to be found those, who were not only by courtesy and designation of office, "Honorable" and "Reverend," but were actually honored and revered as the "stay and the staff" of the community.

The first on its records, and its first President, was James Bowdoin, at the time of its formation the Governor of the State; a Christian gentleman, a ripe scholar, and an incorruptible statesman, who, before his country's independence, incurred the royal displeasure by his assertion of his country's rights; and afterwards for his distinguished attainments in science was counted worthy of a fellowship with the Royal Society of London;* who, to the refinements of letters united a political sagacity and firmness, of which the Commonwealth had full benefit in a crisis of peculiar danger. His administration, alike

* This honor has been very rarely conferred upon Americans. Before the election of Governor Bowdoin, three of our countrymen only had been thus distinguished.

for its integrity and courage, is a stern rebuke to those politicians, of which the race began in his day and has not ceased, who in a time of popular tumult stoop to purchase popular favor at the costly sacrifice of the public welfare and the still costlier, of the permanent respect of mankind.*

Next is Thomas Russell, the first Vice-President, who among the merchants of Boston, confessedly "sat chief;" whose wealth, not of inheritance but of honorable industry, no man could envy who knew of his charities; and whose princely hospitality at once did honor to the city where he dwelt, and was the delight at the time, and the cherished recollection for years after, of the multitude of strangers who shared it. Then follows Dr. John Warren, the trusted physician, remembered of many yet alive, who, with great skill and incessant activity in his profession, combined an ardent zeal for the best interests of humanity. His patriotism, a family virtue, inherited from his fathers, was kindled afresh and kept glowing till his death by the fondness of his fraternal love, and the recollection that a brother's blood was the price of his country's freedom.—Dr. Simeon Howard was the first Treasurer, "an Israelite indeed," whose faithfulness in the little intrusted to his keeping† might well be taken for example by others, holding like dignities, and to whom men have committed much. A patriarchal simplicity engrafted on his intellectual and moral worth never failed of conciliating regard.—We might speak of Dr. Clarke, the first Corresponding Secretary, a polite scholar, a persuasive preacher,

* The following is taken from the records of a meeting of the Trustees, Nov. 8, 1790:—"The Vice-President, Thomas Russell, Esq., communicated an invitation from James Bowdoin, Esq., to attend the funeral of his father, the late Hon. James Bowdoin, on Wednesday next, 3 o'clock, P. M. Thereupon, *Voted*, that the members of the Humane Society be requested to meet at the Massachusetts Bank, on Wednesday next, at half past two, for the purpose of attending the funeral of their late worthy President."

† The funds of the Society were at first very inconsiderable. The condition of membership was the annual payment of a crown, or of one dollar ten cents. But on representation of the treasurer, Dr. Howard, "of the exceeding trouble of *making change*" in the payment of such a sum, crowns having become scarce, the price was altered to one dollar.

and a favorite, alike with the aged, who loved him as a son, and with the young, to whom he was even as a brother. And when we have added to these the names of Lloyd and of Bulfinch, of Dexter and Freeman, of Parker and Lathrop, and of others, the founders or first members of the Society, it will not be difficult to admit, that few companies, civil or military, of laymen or of clergymen, ever passed Castle William, before or since, more worthy of the Governor's salute, than was the company of that day, which was August 5, 1790.

Of the gentlemen thus constituting the first Board of Trustees, many continued in their places for a long series of years. Dr. Aaron Dexter, who, as has been seen, was one of its founders, resigned its presidency in 1827, having been connected with the Society in official relations for nearly forty-two years,—a period far exceeding the usual term of any man's connection with any such institution. Dr. Warren and Dr. Lathrop, also among its founders and first governors, resigned their respective places.—the former as President, the latter as Vice-President, in 1813, after faithful services from 1786, of more than twenty-seven years.

Others also, the immediate successors of the founders, continued in trust through many successive years. The doctrine of rotation in office, with other popular theories, with which it is allied, had not then so obtained as to require that good men, proved to be such, and laden with experience, should *go out*, only that others, not proved, might *come in*. Bishop Parker, Dr. John Eliot, Samuel Parkman, Joseph Coolidge, Esqs., with others, continued to be rechosen from year to year until their deaths, as were also the Rev. Messrs. Emerson and Buckminster; who died, however, at a much earlier period of life. The Society have been favored with the valuable services of many of our leading and influential citizens. Among them may be named Charles Lowell, D. D., Andrew Ritchie. Thomas Handasyd Perkins, John C. Warren, M. D., Henderson Inches, George Hayward, M. D., Jacob Bigelow, M. D., John C. Gray, Samuel A. Eliot, Charles P. Curtis, Jonathan M.

Wainwright, D.D., Charles G. Loring, Abbott Lawrence, Samuel Austin, Joseph P. Gardner, and others. Nor should the long services of the late President, the Hon. David Sears, be forgotten, who for so many years presided over the deliberations of the Trustees and the meetings of the Society, with an impartiality and courtly dignity peculiarly his own.

MEETINGS OF TRUSTEES AND SUMPTUARY LAWS.

The meetings of the Trustees were, at first, on the last Monday of every month. They were soon changed to the first Monday evening of each month, and so continued for almost thirty years. But in January, 1814, when probably the advancing age of some of the members of the Board made their assembling in the day more agreeable to them than in the evening, the hour of meeting was changed to two o'clock; and after the transaction of such business as might occur, the Trustees, together with such guests as their host might have seen fit to unite with them, dined together. The day was subsequently changed to the first Friday of each month; and, ever since 1823, this has remained the stated day. Though the meetings be thus frequent, very few occur without some applications for premiums, or subjects arising, of more or less moment, to call attention. And not seldom, as must be seen in the Catalogue of Premiums, cases of a highly interesting nature and suited to command an earnest sympathy with suffering on the one side, or a warm admiration for heroic efforts on the other, are presented.

We have adverted, on a previous page, to *Sumptuary Laws;* and in recurring to the Records, which, for higher purposes, we have not failed carefully to consult, we find that, at a meeting of the Trustees, at the house of Dr. Spooner, 2d of June, 1826, the following resolution was placed upon the records:—

"*Voted, unanimously*, that if, at any future meeting of the Trustees, there be more than four dishes of meat, fish and soup included, on the table, and two dishes of pastry, it shall be the duty of the presiding officer to order each extra dish to be removed. It being understood that the master of the house be at liberty to determine which those dishes shall be; and that the Secretary furnish each member with a copy of this vote."

The terms in which this salutary regulation is expressed, amounting even to arithmetical precision, would seem to leave little scope to diversity either of opinion or action. But as the interpretation of the article belonged to each individual Trustee, and as no presiding officer, in any remembered instance, found it his duty to interpose authoritatively for the literal enforcement of the act, no effect has hitherto followed, differing at all from what any careful observer of the courses of human society will have learned to expect from all such judicious and well-meant regulations.

MISCELLANEOUS.

We here assemble, under one note, a few separate articles, extracted from the records of different dates, which may show, in connection with the "History," the different objects which have been the subjects of attention with the Society.

It appears that the erection of Light Houses, where greatly needed, sometimes engaged their consideration.

At a meeting of the Society, February 6, 1792, it was

Voted, That the President, the Vice-Presidents, Treasurer, and Corresponding Secretary be a committee to wait upon His Excellency the Governor, and request him to represent to such officers of the government as he may think proper, the necessity of having a Light House erected on some part of Cape Cod, in order to preserve the lives and property of those who navigate the Bay of Massachusetts; and to desire that such Light House may be erected at the charge of the Continent.

Also,

Voted, That the President, Dr. Welsh, Dr. Dexter, and Hon. General Lincoln, be a committee to confer with the gentlemen of the Marine Society, upon the subject to inform them of the measures already taken by this Society, and to request their concurrence in the same.

In the succeeding month, we find the following :—

"The committee appointed to take into consideration the letter from Dr. Thomas Bulfinch, on the method used by the savages for the recovery of persons apparently dead from drowning, reported, that the facts contained therein are a valuable addition to the history of resuscitation, and that it is one of the duties of this Society, to collect every thing of this nature; which, whether founded in reason or experience, should be carefully preserved, and may, perhaps, lead to other discoveries of still greater consequence to the views of this institution. They however take the liberty to remark, that the position in which the savages appear to have placed the body, though doubtless convenient for the discharge of water, must be highly unfavorable to the renewal of respiration."

Here follow some valuable medical suggestions, not necessary, however, here to be repeated.

MEMORIAL TO CONGRESS.

At a special meeting of the Trustees, at the President's, February 23, 1796,

The President informed the Trustees that the Marine Society and the Chamber of Commerce have come to the determination to make an immediate application to Congress, that a Light House may be erected on the highlands of Cape Cod, for the purpose not only of promoting the mercantile interest, but also for the preservation of the lives of seamen, and have expressed their wishes for a co-operation of the Trustees of the

Humane Society to obtain so desirable an end. And the Trustees having taken the subject in consideration,

Voted, unanimously, That a Memorial be presented to Congress, and that Rev. Dr. Clarke and Dr. Dexter be a committee to prepare and report a Memorial on the subject.

Such a document, accordingly, was presented at the following meeting of the Trustees, and having been read and accepted, the President was authorized to sign the same, and to transmit it, through the Corresponding Secretary, to the Hon. Fisher Ames, then one of the Representatives of Massachusetts to Congress. The Memorial itself bears clear evidence of the benevolent spirit, as well as of the classic style of the Chairman of the committee who prepared it, Dr. John Clarke.

JUDGE DAWES'S LETTER.

When the Society, in 1816, had in contemplation a large subscription to the Lunatic Asylum, it was thought that some doubt might arise as to its legal right to appropriate its funds to other than its own original and specific purposes. The President, Dr. Dexter, therefore, sought legal counsel for the direction of the Trustees upon the subject; and the following is the answer received from Judge Dawes:—

BOSTON, 5th Nov., 1816.

Dear Sir:—I think that the last clause of the Act, namely, "And for promoting the cause of humanity by pursuing such means from time to time as shall have for their object the preservation of human life and the alleviation of its miseries," will fully authorize us to proceed with the noble design we have at heart; and I can say most sincerely, that I thank God it is so. The words *may* be construed in a more limited sense, as referring only to those miseries that attend the families of drowned or resuscitated persons. But we are not called to make such a construction. Yours faithfully,

T. DAWES.

DR. DEXTER.

It was in a liberal interpretation of the foregoing decision, and a readiness to co-operate in an object of great public utility, that in May, 1843, a donation was made of five hundred dollars, from the funds of the Society, in aid of the purchase of a costly Telescope for the Observatory established at Cambridge, by the government of the University. "The obvious connection between the discoveries in astronomical science and the diminution of the risks of navigation," seemed to some a sufficient ground for such an appropriation. And, unquestionably, as was urged in its favor, "every advance in the precision and accuracy of all observations of the heavenly bodies, which have relation to time and longitude, is an addition, easily appreciable, to the security of human life, when exposed to the perils of navigation." With equal propriety it might be urged, that the lights of philosophy and the aids of humanity may alike conspire to one great object, "the alleviation of human misery," and that between all good purposes and enlightened efforts there is reciprocal influence. But if, notwithstanding such general reasonings, this particular appropriation should still appear to any a somewhat large interpretation of a discretionary power, the Trustees would not be earnest to contend.*

BENEFACTORS OF THE SOCIETY.

Besides those who, by the devotion of much time and care, particularly in the early periods of the Society, have advanced its general interests, it has not been wanting in liberal contributors to its funds. The following list of donations and bequests has been gathered from the records of successive meetings of the Trustees, or of the Society, through the whole

* The connection between the philosophical instrument, above named, and the designs of a benevolent society, may, however, be closer than by some seems to have been considered. To any ingenuous mind, it will scarcely fail to appear, how naturally a telescope may awaken compassion ; since he, who, looking through it, shall discover with one eye a wreck, too remote for his succor, may weep with the other for sufferings which, though seeing, he cannot relieve.

term of its existence, and it is possible, therefore, that the name of some benefactor may be omitted. But it is hoped that the catalogue will be found essentially correct:

1788.	Hon. Thomas Russell, Vice-President, a share in Malden Bridge, ...	£36 0 0
	With payment of assessment on do., .	2 2 0
1789.	John Calef, Esq., of St. Kitts, two donations,	3 18 0
1790, July 4.	Hon. Thomas Russell, then President, three State notes, together with the gift "of a common seal for the society, engraved on silver,"	311 6 6
1792.	Thomas Dickason, Jr., of London, but residing in Boston, on admission as a member,	6 6 0
	Hon. William Seaver, Kingston, . .	2 2 0
1793.	John Osborn, M. D., Middletown, Conn. .	1 0 0
	Samuel Carey, Esq., of Chelsea, . .	2 13 4
1794.	Jonathan Mason, Esq., first Vice-President,	$ 100 00
	Elisha Doane, Esq., of Cohasset, the furnishing the Society's Huts on Nantasket and Scituate Beach, with all necessary supplies.	
1795.	Madam Thayer, of Boston, a legacy, . .	£50 0 0
	John Bulkley, Esq., of Lisbon, on being elected an honorary member, . . .	$ 100 00
	Thomas Bulkley, Esq., of Lisbon, . .	50 00
1796.	Thomas Russell, Esq., a generous present of a Cabinet, for the use of the Society.	
1797.	Mr. Thomas Hancock, ...	20 00
1799.	Professor Eliphalet Pearson, Cambridge, .	6 15
1800.	Madam Esther Sprague, Dedham, on admittance as a member of the Society, . .	8 90
1801.	Rev. William Walter, D. D., a legacy, .	30 00
1803.	John Bulkley, Esq., of Lisbon, a legacy, .	£ 100 0 0
1807.	Nicholas Gilman, Esq., Exeter, N. H., . .	$ 5 00
1811.	Madam Esther Sprague, Dedham, a legacy,	£ 100 0 0
1812.	Hon. Samuel Dexter, a legacy, . . .	$ 50 00

1822.	William Lambert, Esq., a legacy,	$ 150 00
1823.	Abraham Touro, a legacy,	5,000 00
1831.	Isaiah Thomas, Esq., of Worcester,	300 00
1840.	State of Massachusetts, for building Life Boats,	5,000 00
1841.	State of Massachusetts, for building Life Boats,	1,350 00
1849.	State of Massachusetts, grant,	2,500 00
1852.	State of Massachusetts, grant,	2,500 00
	James Ingersoll, Esq., a legacy,	1,000 00
1854.	Enoch Train & Co., a donation,	200 00
	William Ropes & Co., a donation,	150 00
	James Parker, Esq., a donation,	100 00
	R. B. Forbes, for a friend,	30 00
	G. Howland Shaw, Esq., a donation,	100 00
	Colonel Thomas G. Cary, a donation,	20 00
	Charles W. Morgan, Esq., a donation,	25 00
1855.	United States Government, appropriation,	10,000 00
1857.	United States Government, appropriation,	10,000 00
1870.	United States Government, appropriation,	15,000 00
1873.	Benjamin Hudson, a legacy, which, as Mr. Augustus Lowell, Executor, made no charge for his services, amounted to	22,368 97
1875.	James Alexander, Esq., a donation,	25 00
	Mrs. I. H. Adams,	20 00
	Also, a considerable legacy from the late Mr. P. P. F. Degrand, amounting to one-twelfth ($\frac{1}{12}$th) of the property available after the decease of certain persons now living.	

LIFE BOATS.

It has been seen in the brief "History" preceding, that a grant of five thousand dollars was made by the Legislature of

the State to the Society, in March, 1840, for the purpose of building Life Boats. During the session of the following year, another Resolve was passed, granting thirteen hundred and fifty dollars more, for furnishing three additional Life Boats, to be stationed agreeably to the directions of the Legislature. This sum accordingly was received into our Treasury, and the following Report of the expenditure was presented by the President to the Governor and Council:

To His Excellency JOHN DAVIS, *and to the Hon. Council:*

Agreeably to the resolve of the Legislature of Massachusetts, passed March 17, 1841, allowing thirteen hundred and fifty dollars from the Treasury of the State, for furnishing three life boats, to be stationed as follows: one near Race Point, one at Nantucket, and one at Chatham; I beg leave to report to your Excellency, and to the Honorable Council, that it has been attended to. Houses have been built, and the boats placed therein, and suitable crews appointed by the Selectmen of each town for the purpose of managing them. Finding another boat was absolutely necessary, and being strongly solicited from the town of Plymouth, I prevailed on the mechanics to give in a part of their labor, and build the boats fifty dollars less each, which enabled me to provide a fourth boat for that station, by the Humane Society paying the balance, $175.86, as per account annexed. That boat has been delivered to the Selectmen of Plymouth, who have had a house erected, and men appointed to take charge of her. Thus sixteen life boats are now stationed between Martha's Vineyard and Newburyport, fifteen of them under the direction of the Massachusetts Humane Society, and the one on Plum Island under charge of the Marine Society of Newburyport. And I have the satisfaction to state, that they have already been the sole means, under Providence, of saving the lives of twenty-eight shipwrecked mariners, who otherwise must have met a watery grave, as no other boats could have withstood the heavy sea.

In the gale of the 17th of December last, the ship Mohawk

was cast on shore at Nantasket Beach, when the life boat stationed there was launched into the surf, and, in endeavoring to save the crew, she was driven on the rocks and badly stove. Since which she has been brought to the city and is now repairing, will be finished soon and re-placed in its proper station, the cost of which will be from sixty to eighty dollars. These boats will be constantly wanting repairs, painting, &c. &c., and it will be necessary that a small appropriation should be made for that purpose, subject to the Treasurer of "The Massachusetts Humane Society," the amount to be limited to seven or eight hundred dollars. No more will be drawn for than is actually wanted, and a correct account will be rendered of the expenditure.

I have the honor to be,

Respectfully, Your ob't serv't,

(Signed,) BENJ. RICH,

President Massachusetts Humane Society.

BOSTON, Jan. 11, 1842.

The number of Life Boats and stations has increased from 18 in 1845, to 78 at the present time, a list of the locations of which may be found on the following pages.

The Society have ready another fine boat, (included in the above number,) but its station has not been fully determined.

LIST OF LIFE-BOATS, MORTAR STATIONS AND HUTS OF REFUGE

OF THE

MASSACHUSETTS HUMANE SOCIETY.

MAY, 1876.

No.	Name of Keeper.	Locality.	Salary.	General Remarks.
1	T. S. Greenwood	Ipswich River	$10	One of the oldest boats, built prior to 1840, and not of much use.
2	B. Ellsworth	Near Ipswich Light	10	Small Surf-Boat and Carriage, 1850, moved near the beach.
3	D. Hooper	Annisquam Light	10	Same date as No. 1. Has been repaired, and is in good order.
4	W. Saunders	Lanesville	10	Double-bottom Wadsworth's patent, 1858. Small boat.
5	J. B. Parsons	Rockport	10	Same as 1 and 3, recently renovated. House new.
6	W. Thurston	Rockport	10	Iron Mortar Station, placed 1858.
7	Asa Todd	Emerson's Point, Cape Ann	10	Double-bottom Wadsworth, 1858, lately repaired.
8	Albert W. Hall	Milk Island	5	Hut of Refuge, new in 1873.
9	A. H. Tuck	Gloucester	10	A Wooden Boat, built at Fairhaven, new in 1873.
10	Isaac P. Morse	Stage Fort, Gloucester	10	New Brass Mortar, placed 1872.
11	Charles C. Parsons	Manchester	10	Built at Fairhaven, 1866, removed from Gloucester.
12	John H. L. Giles	Marblehead	10	Built in 1872, Nos. 12 and 13 having been sold. House new, 1872.
14	A. A. Davis	Lynn Beach	10	Surf-Boat, located 1865.
15	Miles Blanchard	Swampscott	10	A fine Boat, by Norcross, 1867.
16	W. Luscomb	Nahant	10	Large clumsy Boat, 1850, newly located 1871.
17	John Hinkley	Deer Island	10	A good Wadsworth Boat, 1857. Brass Mortar and French Apparatus; also, a small Surf-Boat, built in 1850.
18	Joshua James	Stony Beach, Hull		One of the oldest Boats, frequently repaired.
19	Joshua James	Point Alderton		New Boat built at Scituate, and new House, 1873.
20	Joshua James	Stony Beach		Mortar, placed new, 1876.
21	Joshua James	Nantasket Beach	25	Built at Nantucket, 1855, has new floats of rubber, 1871.
22	Joshua James	Nantasket Beach		Hut of Refuge, with stove, &c. Often misused. Burnt April, 1876.
23	Joshua James	Nantasket Beach		Hut of Refuge, with stove, fuel, &c. Often misused.
24	Joshua James	Nantasket Beach	5	New Boat, built at Fairhaven, placed in new House, May, 1872.

LIST OF LIFE-BOATS, MORTAR STATIONS, ETC.—*Continued.*

No.	Name of Keeper.	Locality.	Salary.	General Remarks.
25	Henry Bates	Symond's Cove, North Cohasset	10	Built at Provincetown, 1859, and newly located, 1873.
26	P. C. Kimball	Pleasant Beach, Cohasset	15	Medium size, built 1849, and a Brass Mortar, placed 1871.
27	A. Whittington	Chapel Harbor	10 (27–28)	Large clumsy Boat, built in New York in 1852.
28	A. Whittington	Chapel Harbor		New Boat from Fairhaven, 1871.
29	J. A. Litchfield	Near Glades	10	Good model Surf-Boat, built in Boston, 1856.
30	Charles B. Pratt	North Scituate	10	Medium size, built in 1849-50.
31	J. S. Drew	Scituate, Bass Cove	20 (31–33)	New Boat, built at Scituate, 1872-73.
32	J. S. Drew	Scituate, Bass Cove		Small Surf-Boat, built in 1850.
33	J. S. Drew	Scituate Harbor		New Boat built at Scituate, 1873, to replace Metallic Boat.
34	E. P. Welch	Fourth Cliff, Scituate	10 (34–35)	Medium size, 1852, and Carriage.
35	E. P. Welch	Near last		New Mortar Station.
36	Charles Sears	Cut River, Marshfield	10	New Boat and House, 1876.
36	A. Cushman	Duxbury	5	Small Surf-Boat, 1849. Removed from the beach, 1870.
38	J. D. Churchill	Plymouth	10	A fine Boat, built in 1859.
39	T. Manter	Chiltonville	10	Medium size, built 1849.
40	C. Briggs	Near Manomet Pt., So. Plymouth	10	Nantucket Surf-Boat, 1855, and Brass Mortar, located 1867, locality changed 1876. House new.
41	James Cushman	Near Race Point	10	New Provincetown Boat, built 1870.
42	James Cushman	Near Race Point	10	New Brass Mortar, located 1871.
43	C. A. Cook	East of Race Point	10	New in 1870.
44	C. A. Cook	East of last	10	New in 1870.
45	H. Atkins	Peaked Hill	10	Surf-Boat built at Provincetown, 1852, and Iron Mortar located 1855. 41 to 45 are under the general care of E. S. Smith, Esq.
46	Milford Rich	Newcomb's Hollow, Wellfleet	15 (46–47)	Medium size, 1849.
47	Milford Rich	Newcomb's Hollow, Wellfleet		Iron Mortar, located 1858.
48	Justus Higgins	Cahoon's Hollow	15 (48–49)	Medium, 1849.
49	Justus Higgins	Nigger Hollow		Surf-Boat, 1849, and Hut of Refuge.
50	N. A. Gill	Nauset Light	5	Provincetown Surf-Boat, 1855.
51	Jonathan Snow	Nauset Harbor	40	New Surf-Boat, built near there, 1873, and Iron Mortar, 1855. House fitted for refuge.
52	Elisha Cole	Orleans Beach	10	Surf-Boat, built 1858–9.

53	J. F. Graham .	Wellfleet, inside . . .	15	Surf-Boat and Hut of Refuge, 1867, newly located 1872. Nos. 46 to 53 are under the general charge of Capt. J. Snow.
54	Caleb Nickerson	North Chatham . . .	7	Medium, 1849,—Seldom heard from.
		Chatham		The changes in the harbor of Chatham render the Stations formerly there (Nos. 55 to 59 inclusive) comparatively useless, and they have been given up.
60	From 60 to 71½ are all in charge of Committee at Nantucket, F. C. Sanford, Esq., the Chairman and General Agent.	Near the Bar . . .	60	Medium Boat, 1849.
61		Kroskaty, east end . .		New model double-bank Boat, 1872.
62		Smith's Point West . .		New in 1870. There is a Dory here also.
63		Tuckanuck, West . .		New in 1872. There is a Dory here also.
64		Muskeget, West . .		New in 1873.
65		Forked Pond . . .		Located 1857. Hut of Refuge.
66		Hummock Pond . .		Fine Boat and Hut of Refuge, 1858.
67		North of Sconset . .		Fine Boat and Hut of Refuge, 1858.
68		Great Point . . .		New, and removed from Sconset nearer to Sankaty Light, 1872.
69		In the City . . .		Removed from Sconset, 1870, and repaired.
70		Tom Never's Head . .		New Brass Mortar, located 1871. Iron Mortar, located 1856, and Monitor Raft.
71		Nobedeer		Hut of Refuge.
71½				Hut of Refuge.
72	W. W. Huxford	Chappequidic, Martha's Vine'rd	10	New Station, not complete, May, 1873.
73	Charles Stewart	South Beach, Martha's Vineyard	4	Old Boat, 1849. New House and Floats of Cork, 1873.
74	Asa Smith .	Squibnocket, Martha's Vineyard	15	Old Boat, 1855.
75	H. N. Pease .	Gay Head Light . .	10	Surf-Boat, 1859, and Iron Mortar and Apparatus. Hut of Refuge, &c.
76	S. A. Smith .	Cuttihunk	10	Medium, 1849. 72 to 75 are under the géneral charge of C. B. Marchant, Collector at Edgartown.
77	S. A. Smith .	Cuttihunk	5	Medium, 1850. Near the Light, and very useful and well cared for.
79	Charles C. Church	Cuttihunk	10	Surf-Boat, 1850.
78	Thomas Bates .	Boston Light . . .	5	New Station Boat, built at Fairhaven, and Brass Mortar, 1873.
80	Marcus N. Harris	Barnstable	10	Small Surf-Boat, in charge of Keeper of Light. Iron Mortar.
81	John Flanagan .	Winthrop	10	New Boat and House.
82	Charles Welch .	Sandwich	10	New Boat and House.

CATALOGUE

OF THE

MEMBERS OF THE SOCIETY.

WE subjoin the following List of Members of the Society, which is by no means complete, but the large number here presented, may show the interest taken in the objects of the Society since its foundation, by gentlemen not of Boston only, but of various parts of the Commonwealth.

A.

Samuel Abbot.
President John Adams, *Quincy.*
Isaac Adams, *Orleans.*
Phineas Adams.
Judah Alden, *Duxbury.*
William Alexander.
Jonathan Amory.
Thomas Amory.
Thomas C. Amory.
James Andrews.
John Andrews, *Roxbury.*
Charles B. Appleton.
Nathan Appleton.
John T. Apthorp.
Henry Atkins.
Silas Atkins.
Charles Atkinson.
Jonathan L. Austin.
Richard Austin.
Charles Amory.
William Amory.
John Avery, Jr.
Jeremiah Allen.
Samuel Austin.
William Appleton.

B.

Adam Babcock.
Francis Babcock.
Luke Baldwin.
Thomas Baldwin, D. D.
John Ballard.
Christopher Barker.
Josiah Barker, *Nantucket.*
Thomas Barnard, D. D., *Salem.*
Tristram Barnard.
John Barrett, *Quincy.*
Hon. Josiah Bartlett, M. D., *Charlestown.*
George Bartlett, *do.*
Dr. Thomas Bartlett.
Joseph Bartlett, *Plymouth.*
Dr. Zaccheus Bartlett, *do.*
George Baylies.
Jeremiah Belknap.
John Bernard.
Martin Bicker.
Asahel Bigelow.
Samuel Billings.
James Bird.
Samuel Blagge.
Edward Blake.
Major George Blanchard.
John W. Blanchard.
Elam Bliss.
William Boardman, Jr.
Jeremiah S. Boies, *Milton.*
Kirk Boott.
Ezra A. Bourne.
Hon. James Bowdoin.

John B. Bowen.
John Boyle.
John Boyle, Jr.
Ward Nicholas Boylston, *Roxbury*.
Charles Bradbury.
Gamaliel Bradford.
Samuel Bradford.
Dudley A. Bradstreet.
Major John Bray.
Major John Brazer.
Ebenezer Breed, *Charlestown*.
William Breed.
John Brewer, *Passamaquoddy*.
Thomas Brewer.
Oliver Brewster.
Hon. E. Bridge, *Chelmsford*.
Hon. Matthew Bridge, *Charlestown*.
Nathan Bridge.
Samuel Bridge.
Elisha Brigham.
Andrew Brimmer.
George W. Brimmer.
Henry Bromfield, *Harvard*.
Hon. Peter C. Brooks.
Bartholomew Brown.
Hon. William Brown.
Rev. Joseph S. Buckminster.
Charles Bulfinch.
Caroline Bullard, *Medfield*.
Jeremiah Bumstead, Jr.
Josiah Bumstead.
Thomas Burley.
George Burroughs, Jr.
Rev. Jonathan Burr, *Sandwich*.
Martin Burr.
William Burrows.
Benjamin Bussey.
John P. Bayley.
Nathaniel Balch.
Jacob Bigelow.
Francis Bacon.
John Bulkley.

C.

Hon. George Cabot.
Samuel Cabot, *Roxbury*.
William Cabot, *Watertown*.
Benjamin Callender.
Joseph Callender, Jr.
Thomas Capen.
Samuel Carey, *Chelsea*.
Rev. Samuel Carey.
James Carter.
Edward Cazneau.
Gardner L. Chandler.
Francis D. Channing.
Rev. William E. Channing.
Henry Chapman.
Jonathan Chapman.
Joseph Chapman.
Peter Chase, *Nantucket*.
John Chipman, *Sandwich*.
His Eminence Cardinal John Cheverus.
Asaph Churchill.
Chester Clap.
Benjamin Clark.
Humphrey Clark.
Nathaniel Clark.
William Cleland.
Benjamin Coates.
John Coates.
William Cochran.
Charles R. Codman.
John G. Coffin.
Thomas Coffin.
J. Smith Colburn.
Charles Coolidge, *Newton*.
Charles D. Coolidge, *Roxbury*.
Cornelius Coolidge.
Joseph Coolidge.
Joseph Coolidge, Jr.
William Coolidge.
Zebedee Cook.
Samuel Coverly.
Allen Crocker.
Elisha Crocker.
Edward Cruft.
Andrew Cunningham.
John Cunningham.
Joseph L. Cunningham.
Nathaniel Curtis.
Thomas Curtis.
Charles Cushing.
Charles Cushing, Jr.
Rev. John Cushing, *Ashburnham*.
Hon. Nathan Cushing, *Scituate*.
Hon. William Cushing, *do*.
Thomas Cushing.
James Cutler.
F. B. Crowninshield.
Samuel Cobb.
John Clarke.
Charles P. Curtis.
Caleb A. Curtis.

D.

John Dabney, *Salem*.
Benjamin Dana.
Dexter Dana.
Hon. Francis Dana, *Cambridge*.
Hon. Samuel Dana, *Charlestown*.
William Dall.
Peter Roe Dalton.
Dr. Thomas Danforth.
Benjamin Davenport.
Isaac Davenport.
Aaron Davis, *Roxbury*.
Amasa Davis.
Charles Davis.
Isaac P. Davis.
James Davis.
Jonathan Davis.
Hon. John Davis.
Joseph Davis, *Roxbury*.
Joshua Davis.
Samuel Davis, *Plymouth*.
William Davis, *do*.
Hon. Thomas Dawes.
Major Thomas Dean.
William Dehon.
Benjamin Delano.
Asa Dennel.
Thomas Dennie.
Hon. Elias H Derby, *Salem*.
John Derby.
Aaron Dexter, M. D.
Thomas Dickason, *London*.
Rev. Timothy Dickenson, *Holliston*.
Elisha Doane, *Cohasset*.
Samuel B. Doane.
Samuel A. Dorr.
John Dorr.
Andrew Dunlap.
Alpheus Dunham.
Samuel Dunn.
Isaac Dupee.
Gamaliel L. Dwight.

E.

Samuel Eames.
Charles B. Eaton.
Ebenezer Eaton.
Joseph Eckley, D. D.
Samuel Eliot.
John Eliot, D. D.
Andrew Eliot.
John Eliot, Jr.
Justin Ely, *West Springfield*.
Rev. William Emerson.
John Emery.
William Endicott.
Ephraim Eliot.
Samuel A. Eliot.

F.

Ebenezer Farley.
James Farrar.
Richard Faxon.
John Fenno.
Edward Fettyplace.
James Fillis.
John Fleet, M. D.
Thomas Fleet.
Jeremiah P. Fogg.
Hon. Dwight Foster, *Brookfield*.
James H. Foster.
Henry Fowle.
Hon. Samuel Fowler, *Westfield*.
Ebenezer Francis.
Samuel A. Frazier, *Duxbury*.
Rev. James Freeman.
James Freeman.
Dr. Nathaniel Freeman, *Sandwich*.
Adam French.
John French.
Benjamin Fuller.
Robert B. Forbes.
E. H. Faucon.

G.

Abraham W. Gamage.
Caleb Gannett, *Cambridge*.
Rev. John S. J. Gardiner.
Gideon Gardner, *Nantucket*.
Jared Gardner, *do*.
John Gardner.
Joseph P. Gardner.
John L. Gardner.
Eben Gay, *Hingham*.
His Excellency Elbridge Gerry, *Cambridge*.
J. T. Gilman.
Benjamin Goddard.
Nathaniel Goddard.
Thacher Goddard.
Nathaniel Goodwin.
Nathaniel Goodwin, *Plymouth*.
Ozias Goodwin.
Randolph Goodwin, *Dresden*.
Simeon Goodwin.
John Gore.

Samuel Gore.
Dr. John Gorham.
Moses Grant.
Moses Grant, Jr.
Benjamin Gray.
Edward Gray.
John C. Gray.
Sylvanus Gray.
William R. Gray.
Gardner Greene.
John R. Greene.
James Greene, *Charlestown.*
Richard Green.
Daniel Greenleaf, *Quincy.*
Joseph Greenleaf.
Oliver C. Greenleaf.
David S. Greenough, *Roxbury.*
Rev. William Greenough, *Newton.*
John Grew.

H.

Jared Hall.
Joseph Hall.
Benjamin Hammatt.
Charles Hammatt.
William Hammatt.
William Hammatt, *Plymouth.*
Samuel Hammond.
Ebenezer Hancock.
John Hancock.
Thomas Hancock.
Moses B. Harden, *Medfield.*
Jonathan Harrington.
Edward Harris.
Jonathan Harris.
Rev. Thaddeus M. Harris, *Dorchester.*
James Harrison, *Charlestown.*
Edmund Hart.
Oliver Hartshorn.
Ralph Haskins.
Elisha Hathaway.
Judah Hays.
Caleb Hayward.
George Hayward.
Dr. Lemuel Hayward.
Dr. Nathan Hayward, *Plymouth.*
Joseph Head.
Charles Heard,
John Heard.
John Heard, Jr.
Barnabas Hedge, *Plymouth.*
Daniel Hewes.
David Higgins.
George Higginson.
Hon. Stephen Higginson.
Stephen Higginson, Jr.
Henry Hill.
John Hill.
David Hinkley.
Hon. Benj. Hitchborn, *Dorchester.*
Hon. Samuel Holden, *Danvers.*
John Holland.
John Homans.
Charles D. Homans.
Benjamin Homer.
Charles Homer.
Henry Homes.
Samuel Hooper.
Major Samuel Howard, *Augusta.*
Simeon Howard.
N. Howe.
Abraham F. Howe.
Henry Hubbart.
H. Hollis Hunnewell.
Jonathan Hunnewell.
Augustus Hunt.
Hon. E. Hunt, *Northampton.*
Joseph Hunt, Jr.
Samuel Hunt, *Watertown.*
Rev. Joshua Huntington.
Joseph Hurd, *Charlestown.*
Dr. Isaac Hurd, *Concord.*
Enoch Huse.
Zaccheus Hussey, *Nantucket.*
William V. Hutchings.
Henry Hutchinson.
Ezra Hyde.

I.

Henderson Inches, *Milton.*
Benjamin Ingalls,
Daniel Ingalls.
Daniel Ingalls, Jr.
Dr. William Ingalls.

J.

Edward Jackson.
William Jackson.
—— Jackson, *Plymouth.*
Patrick Jeffrey, *Milton.*
John Jenks, *Salem.*
Joseph W. Jenkins.
John Jenkins.
William Jepson.
Hon. John C. Jones.
Stephen Jones, Jr.
Thomas K. Jones.

Benjamin Joy.
Dr. John Joy.

K.

Oliver Keating.
William Kempton.
Rev. James Kendall, *Plymouth*.
Jacob Kuhn.
John Kuhn.
John King.
John T. Kirkland, D. D.
Josiah Knapp.

L.

Robert Lamb.
William Lambert, *Roxbury*.
Joseph Larkin.
Robert Lash.
John Lathrop, D. D.
John Lathrop, Jr.
Samuel C. Lathrop.
Seth Lathrop.
Stillman Lathrop.
Abbott Lawrence.
Caleb Leach, *Plymouth*.
Ebenezer Lewis.
John I. Linzee.
Hon. James Lloyd.
Robert Lord.
Caleb Loring.
John F. Loring.
Jonathan Loring.
Samuel K. Lothrop.
Joseph Lovering.
Rev. Charles Lowell.
John Lowell.
John Lucas.

M.

William Macey, *Nantucket*.
Henry Mackay.
Mungo Mackay.
John Mackay.
William Mackay.
John Marston.
Hon. Jonathan Mason.
Simeon Mason.
Hon. Ebenezer Mattoon, *Amherst*.
Joseph May.
John May.
John May, Jr.
Samuel May.
John Maynard.
James M'Gee.
Rev. Joseph M'Kean.
Edward M'Lane.
John M'Lean.
Rev. John Mellen, *Cambridge*.
Allen Melville.
Thomas Melville.
Nathaniel Merriam.
Jonathan Merry.
Daniel Messinger.
Henry Messinger.
William Minot.
James Morrill.
Jedidiah Morse, D. D., *Charlestown*.

N.

Joseph Newell.
Samuel Newell.
Charles C. Nichols.
Nathan Nichols, *Malden*.
Perkins Nichols.
George Noble.

O.

James Odell.
George Odiorne.
Ebenezer Oliver.
Edward Oliver.
Francis J. Oliver.
Henry J. Oliver.
Peter Osgood.
John Osborne.
Dr. Cushing Otis, *Scituate*.
Henry Oxnard.

P.

Rev. Asa Packard, *Marlboro'*.
Thomas Page.
Hon. Nathaniel Paine, *Worcester*.
Hon. Robert T. Paine.
William Paine.
Dr. John Park.
Daniel P. Parker.
Rt. Rev. Samuel Parker.
John Parker.
Samuel H. Parker.
Samuel Parkman.
John Parkman.
Francis Parkman.
Charles C. Parsons,
Gorham Parsons.
Nehemiah Parsons.

Rev. Eliphalet Pearson, LL. D., *Andover*.
John Peck, *Newton*.
Ebenezer Pemberton.
Hon. Thomas H. Perkins.
Thomas H. Perkins, Jr.
Augustus T. Perkins.
Henry A. Peirce.
Thomas Perkins.
William Perkins.
Charles Phelps.
Charles P. Phelps.
Hon. Jonathan Phillips.
Hon. John Phillips, *Andover*.
James Phillips.
His Honor William Phillips.
Joseph Pierce.
Nahum Piper.
John Pitts, *Dunstable*.
Joseph Pope.
John Pratt, *Charlestown*.
William Pratt.
Ebenezer Preble.
James Prentiss.
Rev. Thomas Prentiss, *Medfield*.
Samuel J. Prescott.
James Prince.
John Prince, *Marblehead*.
Thomas J. Prince.
Edward Proctor.

Q.

Hon. Josiah Quincy.
John W. Quincy.

R.

William Raymond, 2d., *Nantucket*.
Joseph W. Revere.
Paul Revere.
John Rice.
Benjamin Rich.
John Richardson.
Andrew Ritchie.
Chandler Robbins, *Hallowell*.
Edward H. Robbins.
James Robinson.
Henry N. Rogers.
Thomas Rogers.
Eben. Rollins.
Major Benjamin Russell.
John M. Russell.
Thomas Russell.

S.

Francis Sales.
Samuel Salisbury.
Samuel Salisbury, Jr.
F. C. Sanford, *Nantucket*.
Samuel Sanger.
Daniel Sargent.
Epes Sargent.
Ignatius Sargent.
Samuel G. Sargent, *Charlestown*.
Charles Savage.
William Savage.
David Sawyer.
James Scott.
David Sears.
David Sears, Jr.
—— Sanborn, *Nantucket*.
Dr. Chas. L. Segars, *Northampton*.
Hon. David Sewall, *York*.
Hon. Samuel Sewall, *Marblehead*.
Joseph Sewall,
Robert G. Shaw.
William N. Shaw.
Henry Sheafe.
Dr. William Sheldon, *Springfield*.
William Shimmin.
Andrew Sigourney.
Elisha Sigourney.
H. Sigourney.
Abiel Smith.
Barney Smith.
Benjamin Smith.
George G. Smith, *Danvers*.
Joseph Smith.
Nathaniel Smith.
Samuel Smith.
William Smith.
Samuel Snelling.
Gideon Snow.
Samuel Spear.
Hon. William Spooner, M. D.
Esther Sprague, *Dedham*.
William Stackpole.
Edward Staples.
Zebina Stebbins, *Springfield*.
Hon. William Stedman, *Lancaster*.
William Stephenson.
Robert Stevens, Jr.
Samuel Stillmam.
Thomas W. Storrow.
Juan Stoughton, *Spanish Consul*.
His Excellency Caleb Strong, *Northampton*.
Nathan Sturgis.

Russell Sturgis.
Samuel Sturgis.
John L. Sullivan.
William Sullivan.
Thomas Sumner.
Samuel Swett.

T.

Thomas Tarbell.
Peter Thacher.
Peter O. Thacher.
Rev. Thomas Thacher, *Dedham.*
Dr. James Thacher, *Plymouth.*
Charles Thaxter.
Dr. Thomas Thaxter, *Hingham.*
Minot Thayer, *Braintree.*
Nathaniel Thayer.
Rev. Nathaniel Thayer.
Nathaniel F. Thayer.
Obadiah Thayer, *Newton.*
Samuel M. Thayer.
Dr. Stephen Thayer.
Isaiah Thomas, *Worcester.*
Dr. Joshua Thomas.
Hon. Joshua Thomas, *Plymouth.*
William Thurston.
James Thwing.
Elisha Ticknor.
Jacob Tidd.
Hon. David Tilden.
Joseph Tilden.
B. P. Tilden.
John Tileston.
Samuel Todd.
Samuel Topliffe.
Samuel Torrey.
Eben. Torrey, *Lancaster.*
Abraham Touro.
Isaac Townsend, *Northampton.*
Alexander Townsend.
Russell Trevett.
William Tuck.
John Tucker.
Richard D. Tucker.
Edward Tuckerman.
Edward Tuckerman, Jr.
Rev. Joseph Tuckerman, *Chelsea.*
G. Washington Tuckerman.
William Tuckerman.
Hon. William Tudor.
Daniel Tuttle.
Turell Tuttle.
Hon. Dudley A. Tyng.

U.

Richard Urann.
George B. Upton.

W.

Rev. B. Wadsworth, *Danvers.*
Henry Wainwright.
Rt. Rev. Jonathan M. Wainwright.
Ebenezer Wales, *Dorchester.*
Thomas B. Wales.
Samuel H. Walley.
Lynde Walter.
William Walter.
Hon. Artemas Ward.
Joseph Ward.
William Ward.
John Warren.
J. Mason Warren.
John C. Warren.
Henry Warren, *Plymouth.*
John Waters.
David Webb.
Nathan Webb.
Rufus Webb.
Thomas Webb.
Benjamin Weld.
William G. Weld.
Benjamin T. Wells.
John Wells.
Titus Wells.
Henry A. Whitney.
Thomas Welsh, Jr.
Hon. Oliver Wendell.
Daniel Weston, *Eastport.*
Ezra Weston, *Duxbury.*
Jacob Weston, *do.*
George Wheeler.
Moses Wheeler.
John H. Wheelwright.
Samuel Wheelwright.
Benjamin Whitman.
Davis Whitman.
Kilborn Whitman, *Pembroke.*
Ezra Whitney.
Jonathan Whitney.
Samuel Whitwell.
William Whitwell.
Joseph Wiggin.
Thomas Wigglesworth.
Abraham Wild.
Eliphalet Williams.
Henry H. Williams, *Roxbury.*
John S. Williams, *do.*

John Foster Williams.
John Davis Williams.
Thomas Williams.
William Williams.
Thomas Williams, Jr., *Roxbury*.
Mr. Charles W. Winship, *do*.
John Winslow.
John Winslow, Jr.
Benjamin Winslow.
Charles Winslow.
Isaac Winslow, *Mansfield*.
Thomas L. Winthrop.
Ebenezer Withington.
Elijah Withington.
Abiel Wood, Jr.

HONORARY MEMBERS.

Nathaniel Adams, *Portsmouth*.
Rev. Timothy Alden, *Newark*.
Oliver Baron, *Calcutta*.
Andrew Brown, M. D., *Edinburgh*.
Thomas Bulkley, *Lisbon*.
John Calef, *St. Christopher's*, *West Indies*.
Ammi R. Cutter, M. D., *Portsmouth*.
Anthony Fothergill, M. D., *Bath*.
Hon. Thomas Frazer, *London*.
Hon. Nicholas Gilman, *Exeter*.
Edward Goodwin, M. D., *Bath*.
Dr. David Hull, *Fairfield*, *Conn*.
Hon. Jedidiah Huntington, *New London*.
His Excellency John Langdon, *Portsmouth*.
John C. Lettsom, M. D., *London*.
Dr. John Osborne, *Middletown*, *Ct*.
Hon. Timothy Pickering, *Salem*.
Hon. David Ramsay, *Charleston*, *S. C*.
Dr. Benjamin Rush, *Philadelphia*.
William Russell, *Middletown*, *Conn*.
Hon. James Sheafe, *Portsmouth*.
Rt. Hon. Earl of Stamford, *London*.
Hon. Samuel Tenney, *Exeter*.

Dr. Tedder, *President*,
Leopold Stoger, *Vice-President*,
Alver Roll, *Secretary*, *of the Humane Society*, *of Vienna*, *Austria*.

INDEX.

APPENDIX.

www.ingramcontent.com/pod-product-compliance
Lightning Source LLC
LaVergne TN
LVHW021427110826
845150LV00007B/2113

* 9 7 8 1 4 2 5 5 0 7 8 1 7 *